THE VIRGIN FAMILY
INTERNET GUIDE

WITHDRAWN

THE VIRGIN FAMILY INTERNET GUIDE

VERSION 2.0

Simon Collin

This edition first published in December 2000 by
Virgin Publishing Ltd
Thames Wharf Studios
Rainville Road
London W6 9HA
Version 2.0 – February 2001

ISBN 0 7535 055 2 5

Typeset by Galleon Typesetting, Ipswich
Printed and bound in Great Britain by Omnia Books Ltd, Glasgow

//LET US HELP YOU TO FIND THE BEST ON THE NET

'Look it up on the Internet'

'It's much cheaper on the web'

'Mum, I want my own email'

The Internet isn't just for business people and computer-loving geeks. It's jam-packed with information and things to do for every member of every family. Preschool tots have online games, pictures to colour in and masses of activities. Older kids can hang out in fun, friendly, online clubs or get help with their homework and revision. And parents can use the Internet to manage their finances, book a holiday, get medical advice or just chat about the ups and downs of family life.

The net is great for keeping in touch with friends and relatives. We'll show you how to use email to send news and photos all round the world, how to set up your own family website, how to surf the web like an expert and make sure your family is protected from obscene or harmful material. But best of all, the book has a comprehensive directory of a thousand sites that are fun, useful and friendly for everyone in the family.

Parents are often – rightly – worried about what their children might see or read on the web. And they are also concerned that strangers could contact their children over the Internet. In this book, we explain what the dangers are, show you how to avoid them and spell out the many ways you can make sure that your entire family's online experience is safe, fun and productive.

This book starts with some simple advice about buying equipment and getting online, but it isn't just for beginners. It's also for the millions of people who are overwhelmed or frustrated by the sheer size and complexity of what's out there. We've trawled the web so that you don't have to, and we hope you like what we've found.

Let The Virgin Family Internet Guide be your guide to safe surfing

Simon Collin, who compiled this guide, is a technology writer and net-obsessive who has worked for many of the leading computer magazines and has written over two dozen books about computing and the Internet.

The Internet is evolving so fast that, even though this book was correct at the time of going to press, there could be a few dud addresses or omissions. If you find a site that you think is worth including in the next edition, or if you have any problems with anything in this book, please send us an email at response@virgin-pub.co.uk. We'll make sure it's dealt with in the next edition.

//CONTENTS

10//FAQS – FREQUENTLY ASKED QUESTIONS 224

//GLOSSARY 232

//INDEX 240

//WHAT IS THE INTERNET?

our family's eager to get online but, before you dive in, here's an xplanation of how the different parts of the Internet fit together – nd what they let you do. Using the Internet you can send essages, find homework guides, check your local schools, anage your bank account, get ideas for great days out, chat with hool friends, buy clothes, book a holiday, or read a book. There's othing precise about the Internet and, because it's always nanging and developing, it's hard to define exactly what it does.

he Internet is just a way of linking a lot of computers together so at they can share information. The information is stored ollectively on what are known as 'servers' – computers that do othing else but wait for requests for information, and then supply A server can be a simple PC or a high-powered tower in a special oom. You don't really need to know, since you want to access only e information it stores on its hard disk.

you want to use the Internet and its vast collective store of formation, you need to connect your computer to one of the ervers. You do this using a specialist company called an Internet ervice Provider (ISP). The link from your computer to the ISP is ormally via a normal phone line – you'll need a modem that plugs to your computer and the phone. Once you're connected to the erver at the ISP, you can jump to any of the other millions of ervers on the Internet and see what information they offer.

Vhat you need To connect to the Internet you need a computer nd a modem – a gizmo that links your computer to the phone line nd so connects you to the Internet. To control the modem and the nk you'll need special software (this is normally free and is almost ertainly already part of your operating system). As well as this ardware, you'll also need to subscribe to an ISP – but there are lenty of companies now offering free access.

//THREE BASIC WAYS TO USE THE INTERNET

The Internet is three things at once. First, it's a library o
information you can search and read. Second, it's a way to sen
messages to your friends. Third, it's a way to post messages in
public forum where they can be read by all. Here's a rundown o
the various parts of the net, what they do and what you'll need t
use them.

Internet Access

As well as working to improve the speed of the Internet, th
consumer electronics market has started developing a whole rang
of user-friendly ways to access the Internet without a PC. Standar
domestic telephones have now morphed into complete ema
stations with pop-out keyboard and flip-up screen. And if you ca
operate your TV's remote control, you can surf the web or sen
emails using some of the new interactive digital TV systems such a
Open (www.open-here.co.uk) and Sky (www.sky.co.uk). Flip ope
your remote control to reveal the keyboard and type out you
emails – Internet access was never so easy!

Just about everyone seems to have a mobile phone and these too
are changing rapidly into portable Internet access devices. At the
moment, some phones can access special websites and exchang
email using the WAP (wireless application protocol) system
though it's terribly slow to use. But wait till the end of this year an
the much faster GPRS (general packet radio service) system will b
available; it's much faster and able to cope with sound and eve
video direct to your mobile phone.

The World Wide Web (www or web)

The web is the fast-talking brash salesman for the Internet. It
good-looking, packed with information and very easy to use. Th
web is a great way to present the information that's stored on th
servers connected to the Internet.

The web consists of websites that are run by one person o

company, most of which cover one particular subject. Each website is just a collection of individual web pages – think of it as a library (the web) with books (websites) that are full of pages (the web pages). The difference is that anyone can get published, all the books are linked together and there's a great index that lets you jump straight to any page. On the other hand, the cataloguing has been done pretty haphazardly – hence the importance of search engines (see page 55).

The clever bit about the web is called hyperlinking. Any web page can be linked to any other web page on any other website. A user clicks on a hotspot (that can be a bit of text or a picture) and jumps to the hyperlinked page. This following of links is one of the Internet's most fascinating and addictive aspects – you can wander around for hours and end up finding and reading something great, but maybe totally unconnected to what you started with!

There's a lot of stuff out there and, for many people, when they talk about the Internet they mean the World Wide Web. But, that's just one part of the Internet experience – there's a lot more besides.

Electronic mail (email)

On a day-to-day basis, you'll soon find that the most useful part of the Internet is email. Email is the convenient, free, speedy version of the old postal service. You can send a plain letter – a message – to any other user on the Internet. Automatic systems can even send you a daily message with headlines or sports results, magazine articles or share prices.

In the same way that every server on the Internet has its own unique address, every person on the Internet has their own unique name, combining a user name, selected by you when you sign up for Internet service, and a server name – usually that of the Internet provider or perhaps your company's registered Internet name.

Each day, hundreds of millions of email messages are sent around the world. They are quick to create and delivery to any place normally takes under a minute. For the recipient, it can be very convenient: you can reply to messages in your own time rather than have constant phone calls.

Newsgroups, mailing lists and chat

The web and email are staid and slow in comparison with newsgroups, mailing lists and chat. Each allows users to air their views on any topic that's worth the effort – and plenty that aren't. These parts of the Internet are exciting, but also unruly and, for children, dangerous. Grown-ups will have fun here, but read Chapter 3 to see how best to block out unwanted or pornographic information.

Newsgroups work rather like a big notice board: any user can pin up a message about a new topic or reply to an existing message. All the messages in a newsgroup are stored in public for a few days for anyone to read and comment on what's been said. There are over 60,000 newsgroups that each cover a different topic, whether it's collecting Dinky toys or homework, whether teaching or gardening. You can say or ask anything, get into an argument, get advice or just shout a lot.

Mailing lists are rather more sensible: if you're interested in the subject covered, subscribe by sending your email address. From now on, any subscriber can send a message to the list and it will be automatically distributed to the entire group. It's not an instant forum for chat, but a great way to distribute information.

Chat provides the most dynamic forum on the net. You can join a session and chat about anything to the other people who are there, or use instant messaging to have a private chat with a friend or a stranger.

Extending the system of chat, you can make telephone calls over the Internet – either to a friend connected to the net, or dial out to a real phone. It's a convenient and far cheaper way of making international calls. With the right equipment, you can even see each other.

2//GETTING ONLINE

Before you let the family explore the Internet, you've got to get online. This can be the most difficult part of the whole process – and it normally causes people the most headaches. Once you have chosen a computer, you will also need to set up an account with a company called an Internet Service Provider (ISP), which supplies you with a route on to the net. Next, you will need to install and configure special software to work with this company (although almost all new computers now come with all the software pre-installed, so there you'll face just a few steps before getting online). Finally, you should consider special software to help protect your children from obscene and other unsuitable material on the Internet (this is covered in detail in Chapter 3).

This chapter tells you what equipment you'll need, how to choose it and how to set it all up.

//WHAT SORT OF COMPUTER DO I NEED?

Most computers can be coaxed into going online, but, if you have a computer that's over three years old, you'll find that your Internet provider is unlikely to support the special software you need. If you bought your computer new within the last year, you'll have no problems getting online. If you're shopping for a new system, here are some basic guidelines.

When you buy a new computer, you have two basic choices: do you buy a PC-compatible or a Macintosh? The two options provide different ways of designing what's inside the computer, what sort of central processor chip is used and what sort of software can be run. In practice, PCs dominate through sheer range of software and accessories. Many Macintosh computers look nicer but any extra software or hardware can be more expensive. Software and hardware for one type doesn't easily work on the other platform.

You don't need to invest before you surf. For just a few pounds, your local library provides very cheap access to the net, or, if you want help and a coffee, try a local Internet café.

PC-compatibles Ensure that you're getting Windows 98 pre-installed. You need a reasonably fast processor: anything running at 250MHz or faster will be adequate. The very latest Pentium processor from Intel will speed you along, but from an Internet point of view, a lesser-known chip such as a K6 from AMD will work just as well. You'll need at least 32Mb of main memory (RAM) – most new PCs are supplied with 64Mb. Buy the biggest hard disk you can afford: however big the disk, it'll soon fill up, so ensure you've got at least 4–6Gb on board. Lastly, get a monitor and graphics adapter that can display images at a resolution of at least 800 x 600. (Most web pages are designed to be displayed at this resolution.)

Macintosh Make sure you have System 8 installed (you can make do with 7.5, but anything older is hard work). Any new Mac will be running a PowerPC processor. For those who prefer the Macintosh experience, the price of new Macs – notably the Internet-ready (and cute with it) iMac – has dropped dramatically. Aim for at least 32Mb of main memory – though 64Mb is preferred. Your hard disk should have a capacity of at least 4–6Gb and the graphics adapter/monitor combination needs to support a minimum resolution of 800 x 600 with 256 or more colours.

Going Online with Mobile Phones

The newest breed of mobile phones use WAP (wireless application protocol) – a system that lets you send and read email messages and browse websites. WAP-compatible phones tend to be a little bigger than standard mobile phones, to accommodate the larger display screen and navigation keys. However, the display can still normally only show a few lines of text or very basic black-and-white images.

Each WAP phone and network (Orange, Cellnet, Vodafone or One2One) have different ways of configuring and connecting your phone to the net – you'll need to read the instructions carefully or, better still, ask your phone dealer to set it up for you.

Once you are online, you are limited to the painfully slow connection speed of 9.6Kbps. But still, it's fine for reading short email messages and checking weather, share prices or news headlines. You can't always access standard websites, instead you'll have to start searching for special WAP-sites that have been created using the WML (WAP mark-up language) system. Visit portals such as WAP.com (www.wap.com) and WAP Forum (www.wapforum.com) for a directory of what's available online.

And if you're still deciding whether to get a new WAP phone, you might want to wait until the end of the year when the new GPRS (general packet radio service) system is launched for mobile phones. It will provide high-speed access with sound, colour images and even video direct to your phone.

Fair shares

Most techno-families share one computer between the family, and you'll all want to have some privacy from each other. Your teenage daughter would hardly be thrilled to know that her mother could read her email messages. And the bill payer of the family might want his or her financial portfolio kept out of young Johnny's reach.

One solution is to use a feature of Windows that lets your PC support many different users. Each user has their own section of the main hard disk and can customise the look of the Desktop, install programs, write email messages and browse the web. To set up this feature, click on the Start/Settings/Control Panel menu option. Now double-click on the Users icon.

//HOW DO I CONNECT?

Before you set out to explore, you need to link your computer to the net. Your shopping list has three items on it:

- a box that connects your computer to the phone line (called the modem)

- an account with a company called an Internet Service Provider (ISP), which provides a doorway to the Internet for the public

- a normal telephone line

To get on to the Internet, your modem dials the telephone number of the ISP and connects your computer to the ISP's own large, powerful computer (called a server). The server is your doorway to the rest of the Internet – once connected to it, you'll be able to view web pages, read newsgroups and send email.

Modems

You need a modem (short for modulator-demodulator) in order to convert the digital data from your computer into analogue sound that can then be sent over a standard phone line. The modems also have sophisticated features to cut out any hiss, crackle and pops you might normally hear on a line that would otherwise scramble data.

Slow going

Modems are cheap, work with your existing telephone line and let you connect to any Internet Service Provider. On the downside, they are relatively slow and can take up to a minute to go through the tedious business of actually dialling and connecting to the Internet.

You can get modems tucked away inside your computer (an internal model) or a little box that plugs into the back of your computer (an external model). Both models do the same job – an external model is a little more expensive, and still needs its own electricity socket, but it's easier to move from one machine to another if you upgrade.

Modems are always getting faster. Check that the modem supports software upgrades (often called Flash-ROM or Flash upgrades). Whenever a new specification is developed, log on to the modem manufacturer's website and follow the instructions: new configuration data will be automatically transferred to the modem and it'll run at the new speed.

The lowdown on modems

1   Buy the fastest modem you can. Make sure it supports a
    transfer rate of 56Kbps (the current standard is V.90).

2   Ensure it supports upgrades to Flash-ROM, so you can keep
    up with the latest standard.

3   Some modems include a built-in answering machine. Do
    you really want to pay extra for this? Unlikely.

4   Almost all modems are capable of sending and receiving
    faxes. It's a nice extra that shouldn't cost any more.

5   Internal modems are cheaper, but are more difficult to
    install.

6   Make sure it's BABT-approved (the box will display a sticker
    with a round green spot), which legally lets you connect it
    to your telephone socket.

Faster, faster

Most people connect to the net using a modem, but if you plan to use the Internet every day or have your own busy website to manage, you might consider upgrading to a faster connection.

Each of the following technologies will cost you more than a standard modem connection. You'll need a new box to link your computer to the new communications channel, and the monthly rental is generally higher than a standard phone line. And not every ISP supports these higher-speed technologies.

ISDN (Integrated Services Digital Network) is an all-digital high-speed connection that uses the standard telephone network. It can make the call and connect you to the Internet in less than a second and will outpace even the fastest modem. In the UK there's a big push from telcos (telephone companies) to increase the number of customers (primarily businesses) that connect via ISDN.

Once you have an ISDN line, you need to ask your ISP for a special ISDN dial-up account. Most providers, including the free ISPs, do support ISDN.

Home Highway

Home Highway is a cut-down version of ISDN that's easier to understand, cheaper to install and is still faster than a modem.

If you do plump for Home Highway, you'll need a special ISDN dial-up account from your ISP. Most ISPs, including the free-service providers, will give you ISDN access. But AOL and CompuServe currently don't yet offer this option.

Your old line will be converted to two digital lines (with two numbers) and you'll get a neat box in the corner of your room. Plug in your old phone and your new ISDN Terminal Adapter to connect your computer and you're off. Dedicated surfers will like Home Highway, but there's better technology around the corner.

Cable modem If you have cable TV running into your home, you're looking at the best route to potential high-speed Internet access.

You'll need a cable modem itself (also called a head-end) and a network adapter card for your computer. It'll cost you around £150 for this extra equipment, but you're set up, you have the potential to use the full capacity of the cable. It's a blazingly fast connection from home to net. In practice, you could expect to receive data almost 200 times faster than a standard modem.

The biggest providers in the UK – Cable and Wireless (http://www.cwcom.co.uk), NTL (http://www.ntl.co.uk) and Telewest (http://www.telewest.co.uk) – have all begun to carry out trials in some areas, but you'll have to call to ask when this will happen near you.

DSL and ADSL ISDN's new cousin, DSL (Digital Subscriber Lines), is beginning to appear. It's another way of providing a high-speed digital link to the Internet but its great advantage is that it can work over standard telephone cabling. There are several different versions of DSL technology in place, with one version, ADSL (Asymmetric Digital Subscriber Lines), now a reality in many countries.

ADSL uses a special adapter and your ordinary telephone cable but can pump data along the wire at an astonishingly fast rate. It can send data from the Internet to your computer at a staggering 32Mbps (that's fifty times faster than basic ISDN).

The second main difference is that ADSL is 'always on'; this means that you effectively have a permanent connection to the Internet. For home users, this means no delays when dialling; for business users it means the chance to set up their own server. Instead of paying for calls by the minute, you pay a flat, fixed, monthly rental. In some countries, this is affordable for home enthusiasts, but in the UK the price is set by your ISP and telco and is between £40–150 per month.

The main catch with ADSL is availability. You need to have a local phone company that supports the system and you need to be near the exchange – it supports a maximum distance of around three miles from exchange to home. Lastly, you also need an ISP that supports ADSL (the main business ISPs and many of the larger home-user ISPs all support ADSL).

If you do get set up with ADSL, it should cost no more to install than an existing ISDN line. The terminal adapter will be a little more expensive (around £150) and running costs are built into the monthly rental charge.

Why is it so slow?

The speed of your modem determines how fast you can transfer information to and from your computer. But even with a high-speed modem you could still suffer. You are at the mercy of congestion on the backbone (the motorway that links your Internet provider to all the other providers). As more users log in at peak time, the motorway chokes up – so avoid early evening or your local-time equivalent of when the US wakes up.

Even with a clear run on the main route across the Internet, you still need the equivalent of fast local roads. Your link to your ISP needs to be fast and so does the ISP's link to the backbone. And, if you're trying to view a website, much depends on whether the computer on which the website is stored is fast, its link to its ISP is fast and its ISP has a good connection to the main backbone.

//CHOOSING AN INTERNET SERVICE PROVIDER

An ISP works as a necessary middleman: it provides a local-rate telephone number for your modem to dial in order to connect to its big computers, which form part of the Internet. Only the very biggest sites or corporations link directly to the Internet; everyone else makes use of an ISP and leaves them to manage the techie network connections.

Choosing an ISP can be a problem. Some are vast international companies that are financially and technically solid, provide great support and a good service. Others are two-bit fly-by-nights who could go bust or could ruin your Internet experience by providing a crummy service. To help you choose the right provider, run through the questions on page 15.

> Check that your intended Internet provider supports local-rate calls in your area or you'll end up with a vast phone bill each month. Remember to add the Internet access phone number to your telco's discount scheme, such as BT's Friends and Family plan.

What's the difference between the ISPs? There are lots of different ways of grouping and classifying ISPs, but essentially there are just two types of company: one charges and the other is free. The ISPs that charge are a better choice for businesses and professional users, but are hard to justify for a family. Our recommendation? Go for the free ISP, but choose carefully to make sure that it provides a family-friendly environment.

Free ISPs Some countries, notably the UK, have such aggressive marketing from telephone companies and ISPs that you can now sign up for free Internet access. A free ISP aims its services at home and personal users, and all you have to pay are local telephone charges. In return, you get web space, email accounts, access to newsgroups and free software to get you started.

These companies survive by selling advertising or by splitting the profit on the cost of the phone call with the telephone company. Slim margins, but still profitable.

A couple of ISPs are even experimenting with providing free Internet access and free phone calls. Scour the newspapers for details: they are normally heavily promoted to boost the profile of the ISP and available only at certain times of the week (such as the weekend).

Pros: it's free!

Cons: can be very busy in the evenings and weekends, making it hard to get online. You may have to view more advertisements than with a paid-up ISP and you cannot run a business or create cutting-edge websites – though you can create simple websites.

Paid-for ISPs Many ISPs still charge a monthly subscription fee to connect you to the Internet. For your money (normally between £5 and £10 per month) you get full access to the Internet along with several extra benefits. First, there's no extra advertising – just the plain Internet. Second, you should be able to create a more sophisticated website of your own.

If you're just starting out, you may need to call technical support if your computer refuses to connect. Some free ISPs charge premium telephone rates to reach technical support, but you should receive free 24-hour support from an ISP that is charging you a monthly subscription. Many paid-for ISPs are now realigning themselves to provide e-commerce and other business-related extras.

Pros: free support, rarely hit an engaged tone and the only route to setting up a sophisticated or business website.

Cons: costs.

AOL and CompuServe The biggest ISP in the world is AOL which with its subsidiary CompuServe, has over 16 million subscribers. These two companies take a different route to providing Internet access to subscribers. First, they are both content providers – they have put a huge amount of effort into building up their own private community for subscribers, which is like a mini-Internet with news, sport, music, reviews, games and lots and lots of discussion groups and chat rooms.

In addition to this extra content, you can also use the company's international network of telephone access numbers – which is great for travellers, but not relevant to anyone else.

AOL has some useful features that appeal particularly to families. It has built a range of protection features into its custom software: the parent can create separate accounts (up to five) for different members of the family – and you each get your own email address. The parent can define the type of content that each user is allowed to view. It's a simple, effective way of blocking access to newsgroups, chat rooms and pornographic websites. You can set up any ISP account in this way, but you'll need to buy special filter software (see chapter 3).

AOL has two different ways of charging for its services. Either pay a low monthly subscription, which includes a quota of a few hours online (once you've used up this quota, you'll be charged by the minute), or pay a higher monthly subscription for unlimited time online. To add a degree of confusion, AOL has launched its own free service with Netscape (called Netscape Online, **http://www.netscapeonline.co.uk**). This has all the same features offered by other free ISPs, but it's not the same as the original AOL and doesn't have the custom software, built-in parental controls or other extra features.

//MAKING THE CHOICE

So who's going to get your account? Is it to be a free ISP, or a more expensive content provider or online service?

We've listed the major national ISPs in the Address Book at the end of this chapter. You'll find hundreds of local ISPs near you that offer a good service, but may not have the technical infrastructure to give you the fastest connection to the Internet. Free ISPs are great for home use, but have a limited range of advanced features.

The right ISP for you
Here are some ways to help you choose the right ISP – which one matches you the closest?

1   I'm stingy. Go for an ISP that offers free Internet access
    (see the Address Book).

2   I'm ultra-stingy. Go for an ISP that offers free Internet
    access and free phone calls.

3   I plan to surf only during the evenings and at weekends.
    This is peak time, so you'll have a few busy signals from
    free ISPs.

4   I don't want busy signals. Make sure the ISP has no more
    than ten users per modem (ask them for this ratio when
    you phone for details).

5   I want to connect using Home Highway or ISDN. Most
    ISPs, including the free ones, support this – but ask first
    to make sure.

6   I want each member of the family to have their own email
    address. Make sure that the ISP includes more than one
    email account (often called POP3 accounts). AOL, Freeserve,
    Virgin Net and many others, supply five or more accounts
    as standard, but some provide only one or two.

7   I want to surf till my toes curl. Avoid ISPs that charge by the
    minute. Choose either a free or charging ISP that doesn't
    limit your time online.

//FAMILY PROTECTION

Before you rush out into the Internet, you should be aware of the
potential dangers of the different parts of the net. For example,
your children can easily view violent or pornographic images, read
obscene material or visit unsuitable newsgroups or websites and
can send and receive images via email and can chat to total
strangers with IRC and instant messaging.

To help you manage the fine balance between being a killjoy and
being a responsible parent, use one of the many special protection

rograms available. If you have signed up to AOL, you'll find that its oftware includes a system called Parental Control: the parent can efine what each member of the family can see and do on the net. you have signed up with any other ISP, you will need to buy and stall a protection program (often called a software filter); this ill try to prevent your children gaining access to unwanted ebsites, newsgroups or chat rooms. Chapter 3 has a guide to he different types of protection programs available and how to se them.

GOING ONLINE

o use the Internet you need to install and configure special oftware on your computer. Setting everything up is normally very asy and takes just a few minutes. Best of all, most friendly ISPs will end you a starter pack and CD-ROM when you subscribe with reconfigured versions of all the software you will need. If you on't have a CD-ROM, you can still get online. In any new computer, most all the software you need is preloaded (it's part of Windows r the Macintosh operating-system bundle) – but you will need to onfigure it correctly.

If you can't get online, ask a friend; if your friend can't help, try a local teenager. If they cannot get your system online, try the support line. But watch out: many free ISPs will charge you a premium for this privilege.

---

he info you need

you've subscribed to AOL, CompuServe or an ISP that provides a omplete automated installation package, you don't need to read is section – you're all set to go. But some ISPs will send you a list f settings you need to get online: local phone numbers (called OPs – points of presence) that your modem uses to access the ternet; your preassigned email address; and the 'domain name' f the ISP computer – a series of numbers that uniquely identify very main computer on the Internet (it'll look like '198.122.22.3').

When you set up your Internet connection, the software will probably also ask you to configure your email at the same time. The easiest way to start is to use the email software that's supplied with the web browsers from Microsoft or Netscape. You'll need an email address (see page 20) and more details from your ISP. Most installation programs will automate all these steps for you.

Before you start to configure your computer, make sure that the modem is connected to the computer and telephone socket, and switched on.

Connecting a PC You need to configure Windows so that it knows how to access your ISP. If you are running an older version of Windows – such as 95 or even 3.x, you'll need to follow some extra steps, which are explained in the box on page 22.

Steps to configure your PC

1 Double-click on the Internet Connection Wizard icon on the left of the Desktop. If there's no icon visible, the Wizard icon could be in one of two possible places. First, click on the Start button and look in Programs/ Accessories/Communications. If it's not there try Programs/Internet Explorer.

2 Once the Wizard starts, it displays a welcome screen. Click on the Next button to move through the configuration steps.

3 The Wizard asks what type of new connection you want to create. Choose the middle of the three options to set up this computer to access your own ISP (it's labelled 'I want to transfer my existing Internet account to this computer').

4 Click on the Next button and the Wizard will automatically dial Microsoft and display a list of the ISPs for which it carries details.

5 Choose your ISP from the list and click on the Next button.

Windows will tackle almost all the configuration information required to connect to this ISP – you'll need to type in only your user name, password and email address.

6 If your ISP is not on the list, go back to step 3 and select the last of the three options to configure Windows manually. You'll have to type in the right telephone number and configuration settings, together with your user name, password and email address.

7 You'll also be asked to configure the way in which you read electronic mail and access newsgroups. For these steps, you'll need the name of the mail servers used to send and receive messages (these are sometimes called the SMTP and POP3 servers); their names will look like 'smtp.virgin.net'. To access newsgroups, you'll need the similar name for the newsgroup server (also called the NNTP server); it'll look like 'news.virgin.net'.

8 Once you have entered the information, it is all stored in a file called a 'profile'. You'll find the file in the Dial-up Networking folder in the My Computer icon – just in case you need to make any changes.

The Connection Wizard should have configured your computer so that when you run a web browser, it automatically dials and connects to the Internet. Try it out. If, for some reason, you find that this doesn't happen, double-click on the My Computer icon, open the Dial-up Networking folder and double-click on the connection profile you created in the previous steps. This should connect you to the net.

Your best support channel is probably that geeky, netwise friend that you've been patiently buttering up for years. Just make sure he really does know what he's talking about.

Connecting a Macintosh to the net If you have a new Macintosh that's running System 8, you'll get plenty of help from the Internet Setup Assistant. It takes you step by step through the process of configuring your Mac ready for the net. If you have an older machine, look to the box on page 22.

Steps to configure your Mac

To get started, you'll need the list of settings from your ISP.

1 Double-click on the Internet Setup Assistant icon
 (or choose the Internet Access option from the Apple
 menu, then select Internet Setup Assistant).

2 Click on the 'yes' option to set up a new Internet account.

3 You'll follow through a series of simple screens, each of
 which asks you to enter one of the bits of information
 supplied by your ISP.

4 Once you've finished, your Mac is configured. You're ready
 to go online.

The Setup Assistant should have configured your computer so that, when you run a web browser, it automatically dials and connects to the Internet. If you find that this doesn't happen automatically, choose the Remote Access Status option from the Apple menu to make the connection.

Choosing an email address

When you sign up with an ISP you'll be asked to choose an email address that will be unique to you and used by your friends to send you messages.

When you choose your email address, you'll probably type in your first name and surname. For example, if you're signing up for Freeserve, you might type in 'john@smith. freeserve.net'. You can bet your bottom dollar that your name has already been assigned to someone else. The ISP will suggest an available address like 'john@smith72. freeserve.net' – but you could try a few alternatives to get a really unique address. You could try 'john@smith_family' or, as you get more desperate for a unique name, even your hobby, nickname or house name.

Am I connected? If you double-click on the web-browser icon on your desktop, this will automatically start the Windows program that dials the ISP's access number and connects your computer to their bigger computer, which in turn provides the doorway to the Internet. First of all, you'll see the Dialer tell you it's trying to dial the ISP's access number. Once it's connected, the Dialer window disappears and the web browser window appears. You're now online – that is, connected to the net.

When you're online, Windows 98 displays a tiny icon in the bottom right-hand corner of the screen (next to the time) with two tiny green squares linked. If you see this, you're online. The squares should flash bright green to show information is being transferred. The top square is the distant computer at the ISP and the lower square represents your computer.

To check if your email system works, start your email program and click on the icon or button to send and receive mail or check for new mail. It should start the Dialer automatically, connect to the Internet and contact the post office server at your ISP. If you get to this stage and you see an error message, you've entered either the wrong address for the post office or the wrong name and password. Check all three and try again.

Test your email connection: send us a message and we'll send a reply straight back! Type the 'To' address as 'test@virgin-pub.co.uk' and click on the Send button, then the Send/Receive button. The email software will connect to the Internet and send the message. Wait a minute or two, then click on Send/Receive again to pick up any new mail.

Not working yet? In case you're having problems getting online, here are some of the common problems that beset new users.

1 When you start your web browser, does a window pop up (called the Dialer) to tell you the software is dialling and trying to connect to the net? If not, connect manually (see the 'Steps to configure ...' sections above).

2 When the Dialer pops up, does it say 'Dialing'? If not, there's a problem with your modem or modem settings. Make sure the modem's on and plugged in.

3 If the Dialer tells you there's 'no answer', make sure that you entered the access telephone number correctly.

4 When the Dialer connects, it displays a message that it has connected. Next, it sends your user name and password. If you see 'Authorisation error' or similar, there's a problem with your user name or password – they are case-sensitive (in other words, they differentiate between capital and lowercase letters), so enter them carefully.

Connecting an older computer to the net

If you have a computer that uses Windows 3.x or a Macintosh that uses System 6 or earlier, it's rather more difficult to get online. You'll have to use older software that lacks the friendly touch of the latest Wizards and Assistants.

If you are still having problems and your ISP can't help to find suitable software, you have two choices. You could visit a local Internet café or your library and spend an hour searching a site such as CNET (http://www.cnet.com) or TUCOWS (http://www.tucows.com) for suitable software. As a last resort, you might have to consider upgrading your computer so that it can run one of the newer operating systems. If your computer has 16Mb or more of memory and a Pentium or PowerPC processor, you should be able to

upgrade the main operating system to Windows 98 or
System 8 (for PCs and Macs, respectively).

Setting up your email program

If your ISP didn't supply a friendly installation program or you didn't
use the Wizard or Assistant to do the hard work for you, you'll
need to set up your email program yourself. You'll find it easier to
start by using the email program supplied with your web browser –
you can always change later to a different program (where the
setup process will be very similar).

1   Open your web browser. To start the email program,
    choose the Go/Mail menu option if you're using Microsoft's
    IE, or Communicator/Messenger Mailbox in Netscape. This
    starts a separate program: Microsoft Outlook Express or
    Netscape Messenger.

2   You need to open the setup screen: in Microsoft's Outlook
    Express, this is under Mail/Options; in Netscape Messenger
    it's under the Edit/Preferences menu.

3   The program will ask you to enter your own email address
    and password (normally the same as your standard Internet
    password) and the names of the two email servers supplied
    by your ISP.

4   Once you have typed in all four pieces of information, you
    are ready to send and receive messages.

//ADDRESS BOOK

Major ISPs

*There are hundreds of other ISPs – some small, local companies,
others offering national coverage. These companies will set you
up with an account for a monthly payment; each provides basic
dial-up access for users with modems but can scale up to*

businesses with high-speed ISDN links or specialist requirements.
This modest range of ISPs includes some of the larger companies
that have been providing Internet access for several years. Look
in an Internet monthly magazine for full listings.

AOL 0800 376 5432	**http://www.aol.com**
BT Internet 0800 800 001	**http://www.btinternet.com**
CompuServe 0990 000 200	**http://www.compuserve.com**
Demon 0845 272 2666	**http://www.demon.net**
Direct Connection 0800 072 0000	**http://www.dircon.net**
Easynet 0845 333 4000	**http://www.easynet.net**
Global Internet 0870 909 8042	**http://www.global.net.uk**
IBM 0990 426 426	**http://www.ibm.net**
Netcom 0990 668 080	**http://www.netcom.net.uk**
Pipex/UUnet 0845 088 4455	**http://www.dial.pipex.com**

Free ISPs

Getting in touch with free ISPs by phone is hard work – they like
to give out only the numbers of premium-rate support lines. For
BTClick, call the operator and ask BT to send a CD. For Freeserve,
visit Dixon's or PC World. X-stream and LineOne expect you to
download their software from their website. Virgin Net will send
you a welcome pack and CD.

BT Click	**http://www.btclick.com**
LineOne	**http://www.lineone.net**
Netscape Online	**http://www.netscapeonline.co.uk**
Virgin Net	**http://www.virgin.net**
Freeserve	**http://www.freeserve.co.uk**
X-stream	**http://www.x-stream.co.uk**

3//NET WORRIES

Because of its history as a forum for uncensored, free speech, there's plenty of unpleasant material out in the big bad Internet – and most parents would rather that their children didn't find out about it just yet. How can you stop your children viewing pornography and other unsuitable material? And do paedophiles really lurk around chat rooms? And once you have made your Internet connection child-friendly and safe, what worries are there about the computer itself? Will it damage their eyes, give them RSI or even cancer?

This chapter provides straightforward answers to all the main problems and worries parents have when they let their children on to a computer linked to the Internet.

//CHILD SAFETY ONLINE

The Internet is not always a friendly or safe place for children to explore – there are plenty of dangers, from easy access to obscene material through to harassment or child abuse. However, in this respect it's no different from real life and to ban your child from using the net is a blinkered view. Far better to take time to protect them as much as you can, but also to explain the dangers to your kids and ensure that they are net-smart.

Newspaper and magazine articles tend to concentrate on scare stories and problems regarding the web and the mass of pornography that's freely available. In fact, this is just one small problem and relatively easy to deal with: you can block access to obscene material effectively by using software filters that prevent your child visiting certain sites. Oddly, pornography has also been responsible for fuelling – and paying for – much of the growth in new web features including e-commerce, video and multimedia technologies.

The less obvious source of problems tends to be interaction with other users – particularly via online chat. Teenagers will want to hang out in online clubs and chat to pals and other teens about life and stuff. But it's very hard to be sure that you know who's at the other end of a chat session.

Although, thankfully, they are very rare, there are now occasional cases of children being followed or harassed online, or in real life, after chatting to a new 'pal'. Since there's no way of checking the age or identity of anyone online, their new friend could easily turn out to be a forty-year-old weirdo. It's sometimes hard to block or detect these problems, but you can do several things to make sure your children act responsibly, understand the dangers and take care with online chat.

Here's how to make sure that your computer and Internet connection are safe and friendly for the whole family.

It sounds draconian, but a good system is to draw up a mini-contract for use of the Internet: the children agree to various basic rules for using the Internet and in return they get time online. If they break a rule, they lose time online.

Blocking access

As we've seen, one of the best ways to ensure that you protect your kids from unsuitable material – in websites, email messages or newsgroups – is to install a special software filter program. Once it's been loaded, the program sits in the background and monitors and limits what your children can do. The programs use two methods to block access

Blacklisted sites Some software filters use a huge list of unwelcome sites and block access to them if your children type in a site address in their web browser or try to access a newsgroup via a news reader.

You'll need to download regular updates from the Internet so that the software's always up to date with the latest nasties. Once it's installed, you can configure the program and add any extra sites you particularly want to block – and even prevent access to search engines and directories that list unsuitable and obscene material, instead limiting your children to the excellent and safe Yahooligans! (http://www.yahooligans.com) directory.

Blocking keywords Some software filters work by detecting keywords rather than using a block list of unwanted sites. They check what's been typed into any search engine, and also what's being displayed, to block sites that include words like 'sex' and also prevent your children typing in keywords. The more advanced filters include a degree of intelligence so that they will allow users to search for or view sites about 'chicken breasts' but not 'big breasts'.

The advantage of these keyword programs is that they can work seamlessly across the entire range of Internet software – including the special programs used for chat and newsgroups.

PICS – standards for blocking websites

PICS (Platform for Internet Content Selection) is a standard that helps rate websites by allowing designers to include information within their web pages that explains what's inside. For example, a site about teddy bears might include PICS information that their site is very safe for all ages, whereas a men's fashion magazine might rate itself as including some bad language and nudity and a hardcore 'adult' site would carry data rating it as suitable only for grown-ups.

To use this PICS information, you need either a compatible web browser (such as Microsoft Internet Explorer or Netscape Navigator) or a software filter (see below). Either program will let you define the type of site that can be viewed or type of material you want to allow.

Since some sites may not add this PICS rating information or may put in the wrong type of rating, you should use ratings created by an independent third party (such as RSACi at http://www.rsaci.org or SafeSurf at http://www.safesurf.com).

Microsoft's IE browser lets you experiment relatively easily to set up different levels of filtering – choose the Options/View/Security menu command and select which categories you want to block with the Content Advisor settings. To use PICS filtering with Netscape's Navigator choose the Help/NetWatch menu command: this will connect you to the Internet and ask you to register and fill in details online before configuring your browser.

The problem with this system is that it relies on the websites including the information; so far, few do. If the site doesn't include the rating information, it won't be blocked.

Software filter programs We've seen what they can do. Now let's look at some of the filter programs themselves.

There are dozens of different ones, which work in the background to help protect your children by blocking unwanted sites. Get advice and instruction on protecting your connection with the WorldVillage Parental Guide (http://www.worldvillage.com/wv/school/html/control.htm). You can also view a complete list of the filter programs at the same address. Alternatively, here are the sites for the most popular filter products – you can download a demonstration copy to see if it fits your requirements:

Cyber Patrol   http://www.cyberpatrol.com
Keep the kids in the safe zone by installing this rival to NetNanny – set up restricted zones to prevent kids from visiting X-rated sites.

Cybersitter   http://www.cybersitter.com

Blocks sites according to a vast list of sites that contain obscene, hate or antisocial material.

NetNanny   http://www.netnanny.com

Top-selling utility that prevents your children from visiting X-rated or antisocial websites and newsgroups.

SurfMonkey   http://www.surfmonkey.com

Creates a cheerfully controlled environment with its own browser that restricts what kids can do and where they can visit.

SurfWatch   http://www.surfwatch.com

Monitor and limit the areas your children visit on the net.

Safe web surfing

As we've seen, if you subscribe to AOL, you can use the Parental Control option to control which sites and newsgroups can be viewed by the other family accounts. Non-AOL surfers can use a commercial program that can be set up to prevent access to a vast list of obscene sites (or spot and block obscene words), such as NetNanny (http://www.netnanny.com), Cyber Patrol (http://www.cyberpatrol.com) and SurfWatch (http://www.surfwatch.com), which all provide a good degree of protection.

Even after you have installed a filter to block access to obscene sites, there's still a chance that your kids will see unsuitable material – it's impossible for the software manufacturers to keep up to date with every new unwelcome site. Make sure that your children are net-smart and understand what's out there, why it's dangerous and why you don't want them to view it. This is part of a trusting relationship between you and your children. After all, a child can see naughty pictures by strolling into any newsagent.

We've already discussed the idea of a sort of mini-contract with your child. This would lay down the rules for using the Internet safely in return for time online. If the child breaks the agreement, you cut the time online. To help you get started, there's a printable online Agreement (though you'll probably want to edit and change bits to suit your style) at the excellent general-resource centre protecting kids online: http://www.cyberangels.org.

Safe chatting

Online chat rooms are, generally, full of adult content. Swearing is often the normal form of greeting and the subjects can be very adult. Most parents have no idea of the dangers of online chat – but they can, potentially, be far worse than websites.

One of the major problems is lying. Doesn't sound too bad, but watch out. If your child enters a chat room and someone tells them she's ten and loves netball, you've no idea if this is true or if it's a bearded hacker out for some twisted fun.

Similarly, it's very easy to extract information from someone about movements, name and location without actually asking directly. In a chat room, someone might just say, 'Hi, my name's John. What's yours?' After a few minutes' chat, they might ask if you like school, mention your school's name and you've given them a location. Give your age and they'll know your class. Tell them your parents work and they'll know the house is empty. And so on.

As a parent, you should be very, very wary of any type of chat site. If you're using AOL, make sure that you've used the Parental Control panel to set up the type of chat room that your kids can visit. If you're not on AOL, use a filter program that warns against adult-themed chat rooms. However, the best advice is in three parts:

• Set up a pact or contract with your child – they have to check with you before using a chat room or they'll lose surfing time. Most of the software filter programs can keep track of when someone's last used a particular program (like a chat program), so it's not hard to monitor.

- Make sure that you either visit the chat room first or sit with them for a time to see what's going on.

- Warn your child about giving out private information. Draw up a list together: never give out your address, phone number, school or similar details. For some scare stories to drive the point home, visit http://www.parentsoup.com.

Safe email

Children are just as much at risk when using email as when browsing the web. Some dangers are mild, such as unwelcome advertising messages via email; others unwanted, such as pornographic images attached to messages; or even upsetting, such as anonymous hate messages.

There are plenty of ways to protect your children when using email. Some ISPs automatically block out incoming advertising messages (generally called 'spam') – ask your ISP for their policy on this. AOL provides its own custom software to access email, and includes a Parental Controls feature that lets the parent define what their children can do with email. For example, you can prevent the child accessing attachments (files that may contain images), or block certain email addresses. Many of the software filter programs, such as Cyber Patrol and NetNanny, can block attachments and include features to block all incoming mail except messages from known friends.

If you plan to use newsgroups or any form of chat, you'll need to give out your email address. Once you publish your email address in any of these public forums, you are likely to receive spam or unwelcome messages. The best advice is to use a dud email address (see page 84) and give this out instead. This way, messages sent to the dud address are simply returned to the sender as undeliverable.

Make sure that your children understand the risks. Try to follow these key guidelines for children:

Children should:

- set up a new, dummy email address if you allow them to use Internet chat

- tell their parents immediately if they receive an anonymous, obscene or hate mail – the parents can then ask the ISP to trace the source and block it

- be very cautious before opening any email attachments – they could contain viruses or obscene material

Children should never:

- give out their email address to a stranger

- respond to any suggestive or obscene messages posted on a newsgroup or discussion group

- arrange a meeting with a stranger via email

Safe newsgroups

An uncensored soapbox like Usenet can get pretty warped. A lot of the postings are crude or obscene, and can include pornographic image attachments. It's not really the place for young, impressionable minds to go exploring. However, only a few groups are truly offensive and, as a parent, you might want to block all newsgroups for young children, but block only a few unsuitable groups for teenagers.

Newsgroups are arranged into categories called hierarchies. These give you a clue as to the type of content of the newsgroup. The first part of a newsgroup's name is its hierarchy category (so comp.ibm.pc is in the 'comp' hierarchy). The 'alt' hierarchy is by far the wildest in terms of uncensored and unsuitable content. However, if you block all of the 'alt' newsgroups, you'll also miss

...ut on masses of hobby and enthusiast groups. To avoid most of ...e pornographic images, block any newsgroup with 'pictures' or ...inaries' in its name, together with all the 'alt.sex' newsgroups.

...you subscribe to AOL, there's no problem – use your Parental ...ontrol page to limit which newsgroups your children can view. ...ternatively, install a product such as NetNanny or Cyber Patrol, ...hich, as we've seen, limit access to obscene newsgroups and ...revent children typing in or reading material that contains ...bscene material.

...more dangerous side effect of using newsgroups is that you have ... give your email address when your write (or 'post') a message. If ...our child uses their main, real email address you can guarantee ...at they will receive unwanted advertising messages – or worse – ...ithin a few days. The solution is to use a made-up email name or, ...you really want to get messages, set up a free email account (see ...age 70) and use this when posting to newsgroups.

... help maintain a few standards of decency, some newsgroups ...e moderated: one person keeps an eye on the postings to make ...ure it's up to your standards or level of decency as well as his. ...loderated groups are normally free of crude idiots and spam, and ...enerally provide lots of answers and good discussions on a ...hole range of topics. But it can be hard to find a moderated ...ewsgroup: there are fewer than 300 out of the entire 60,000 ...nge. Most have names that end in .moderated, .info, .answers, ...esearch, or .reviews.

...rivacy

...any Internet companies have ways to gather data about you that ...ey can later use for various reasons. It is very easy to give out ...formation over the Internet about you, your family and your ...ovements without considering the implications. Children in ...articular should be careful not to give out personal information.

Plenty of commercial websites ask for personal information i
exchange for a customised web page or other service. They use th
to help them plan marketing campaigns and promotions. If yo
modify a portal, such as Excite! or MSN, you're typing in valuabl
marketing information – but it's not particularly dangerous. Som
online shops will sell your personal details on to other companie:
and you're then likely to get a barrage of 'spam' email advert
Before you shop or enter your personal details at any site, rea
their privacy statement. If they don't have one, move o
somewhere else.

It's surprisingly easy for children to give away name, age – eve
their school or phone number – during the course of an email c
chat conversation. They shouldn't – they could be giving
potential loony the information to harass or even stalk them.

Some software filter programs, such as Cyber Patrol, can watch ou
for keywords and block them before they are transmitted. Th
parents can set this up so that it will prevent their child sendin
their address, surname or school name.

If you think you're anonymous when you're on the net, just visit
http://consumer.net/anonymizer/ and see how much personal
information you're already showing in public.

The threat of a virus
Almost any file that you download from the Internet could contai
a virus, but the number of incidents is very low. Most viruses lur
inside a program file but, more recently, Word documents hav
started to carry bugs. A virus is a nasty but very clever little prograr
that burrows deep inside another file. When you open or run th
carrier file, the virus wakes up and does two things: first, it tries t
spread to other similar files – to 'infect' them – and next, it may tr
to wreak havoc on your computer. Many viruses are benign an
simply spread themselves, but the majority will try to delete files
crash your hard disk or corrupt information stored in files.

It's important to remember that you cannot catch a virus simply by downloading a file. However, if the file you download is infected with a virus, you will catch it when you open or run the file. If you download a file or receive a file via an email attachment, it could contain a virus. Only a few types of file can't contain viruses: notably image files and plain web pages (however, many web pages use extra programs, called applets, to provide multimedia or special effects – and these could contain a virus).

To stop any potential problems, you should always scan newly downloaded files with a special software program that can detect and remove viruses. Two of the most popular virus detection programs are McAfee (http://www.mcafee.com) and Norton AntiVirus (http://www.symantec.com).

New viruses are being developed by eager hackers, so you will frequently need to download special update files to ensure your antivirus software can catch all the latest strains.

//STAY HEALTHY!

Are you sitting comfortably? Don't slouch! And sit up straight! Great advice both for sitting down for dinner and in front of the computer, but often made more difficult with a poor choice of chair, desk and lighting. When arranging your computer, desk and chair for the family you should try to make it a comfortable, flexible place to work that can be easily changed to suit tall Tim or small Susan.

When you use your computer, it's not acceptable to expect a little backache, a headache or sore wrists. Lots of people put up with these problems, but it takes just a minute to plan your computer installation so that you don't suffer with any of these complaints.

Your aim is to set up the chair and desk so that when you sit ready to use the computer:

- your feet are flat on the floor
- your knees are slightly higher than the bottom of the chair
- your elbows form a 90-degree angle and are close in at your sides (this will mean that your forearms are parallel with the floor)
- your wrists are straight when typing or using the mouse
- your eyes are a little above the top of the monitor
- the monitor is about two feet away from you

Since everyone in the family is a different shape and size, it's worth investing in a chair that can be adjusted and, if you have small children, a foot stool to make sure that their feet aren't dangling in midair (causing lower-back strain). Here are some of the most important points when planning an ergonomic, comfortable place to use your computer.

Do make sure that everything (chair, desk, footstool) can be adjusted for each member of the family, or buy separate chairs – and make sure that you make the adjustments!

Do adjust the chair height so that you are sitting comfortably and your wrists are straight when you type. If the keyboard is too thick use a padded wrist rest to raise the level of your wrists.

Do use a desk or table that's designed for work, not eating. A desk for an average (175cm tall) person should be around 70cm off the ground.

Do make sure that the monitor is around 60cm away from your eyes and that the top is just below your eyes.

Don't use straight-backed kitchen chairs – they are the wrong height and not comfortable.

Don't let your feet dangle in midair (chair too high) or cross over or the floor (chair too low). Either use a foot rest or adjust the height of your chair and desk.

Don't put your monitor in front of a window. It's nice to look out at the view, but the bright light will strain your eyes.

Don't ignore any pains, tingles or aches – something in the setup is not adjusted correctly.

Avoiding eye strain Tired, watery, stinging eyes are the worst symptoms when you overuse your computer. Any activity that involves concentrating on a fixed point just a few feet away from you for a long period of time will strain your eyes. You won't go blind staring at a screen, but you can easily get headaches and eye strain unless you follow a few simple rules.

- If you have a long report or games session to finish, try to look up and out of a window for a few minutes every half-hour. This relaxes the muscles that focus your eyes on the screen.

- If you wear glasses, make sure that the prescription is up to date – staring at a screen multiplies the effects of the wrong prescription. If you wear bifocals, make sure that you can see clearly out of one of the segments or order a special pair of glasses for close work with a computer.

- If you're planning to use the computer all day, use remoisturising eye drops (especially if you wear contact lenses). When you stare at a screen, you blink less and your eyes will dry out, causing itching and stinging.

- Many websites – particularly the online games sites – use a tiny character size for text. Use the menu options in your browser to increase this (View/Text Size in IE and View/Increase Font in Navigator).

Tingling fingers and RSI If you're using your computer for hours at a time, particularly if you sit badly or are typing out a long report or playing games using a mouse, you are in danger of suffering from the modern malady, RSI (repetitive strain injury). RSI normally makes itself known in your wrist and forearm, but you can also suffer similar injuries in your neck, spine, elbow (tennis elbow) or knee (horseman's knee). By following a few basic guidelines you can diminish the risk of RSI dramatically.

The most common form of RSI is often called CTS (carpal tunnel syndrome). If you feel something similar to pins and needles or get a burning sensation in your wrists or the inside of your forearms, your computer, desk and keyboard are probably in the wrong positions and, unless you rearrange your working environment, you could easily end up with the first stages of RSI.

Children who can't touch-type are likely to suffer a sore neck – they tend to look up and down between keyboard and monitor as they type. Similarly, children who play video games using a mouse for hours on end, can easily find they have sore wrists and the possibility of the first stages of RSI.

CTS occurs because the main median nerve that runs along the inside of your forearm, through your wrist and to your hand is being squeezed by an inflamed tendon or cartilage (as a result of being irritated by the repetitive action of typing or clicking a mouse). Follow a few basic precautions and you will prevent a very painful injury.

- Make sure that your keyboard and chair positions are adjusted for your height. Adjust your chair so that your forearms are parallel to the ground and your wrists are flat. Use a padded wrist rest if your keyboard is too thick.

- Stretch and flex your hands and wrists every half-hour: make a tight fist, hold for a second, then stretch your fingers out for a count of five.

- If you or your children are prone to cold hands (or poor general circulation), you can help by drinking water just before you hit the keyboard – but avoid coffee or caffeine-based soft drinks that dehydrate.

- Ask your doctor for advice if you have repeated aches or your fingers tingle (as if with pins and needles) for a long period of time.

Electronic emissions Your computer and, particularly, your monitor create a whole range of electronic emissions but these are no worse than a television or most other electronic equipment at home. There are plenty of scare stories that suggest there's an increased risk of cancer and miscarriage, but so far nothing's been proven. However, rather than take a risk, follow these simple precautionary guidelines.

- Position your monitor so that it's as far away as possible – but still legible without eye strain (see page 36 for more information).

- The emissions are worse on the sides and back of the monitor, so don't put the monitor across the kitchen table from your sister or brother.

- If you are using an old or faulty monitor, upgrade it. Newer models have far better shielding to prevent excess emissions escaping outside the casing.

4//SURFING THE WEB

The web is the part of the Internet that gets all the attention – it [is] easy to use, pretty to look at, full of exciting gimmicks and can b[e] incredibly useful. You can get help with your homework, chec[k] sports results (or watch the match), listen to music, read books[,] shop till your credit card expires, scan the news and weather or d[o] just about anything you choose – with a click of your mouse.

//WHAT IS THE WEB?

The World Wide Web (WWW) is a collection of millions of individua[l] websites. Each site is made up of individual web pages – compute[r] files stored on a server that tell your computer what to display o[n] screen. The Virgin Publishing site (http://www.virginbooks.com[)] for example, contains hundreds of web pages, each of whic[h] might be about a particular book published by Virgin.

Web pages are written in a computer language called HTML [–] HyperText Markup Language. One of the clever things about HTM[L] is its hyperlinks or links – with which the page designer can defin[e] text or pictures as 'hotspots'. So, when you click on a hotspot, yo[u] jump to another page on the Internet or to another point on th[e] page. Links are normally displayed as coloured, underlined text bu[t] are sometimes behind photos or other images. When you mov[e] your mouse pointer over a hyperlink, it changes shape from a[n] arrow to a pointing hand. Click on a hyperlink and the new page [is] displayed.

A page can also include graphics, sound or video clips – these ar[e] all stored in separate files and referenced using HTML command[s] (see chapter 8 for more details on HTML). Each file has a name an[d] usually ends with the file extension 'html' – like 'news.html[']. Sometimes, pages have an 'htm' extension – but it means the sam[e] thing. If you see a page ending 'asp' (for example, 'news.asp'), you're seeing a special kind of page that is filled with information only just before it is displayed.

Sites and home pages

A website is a collection of web pages that stands on its own. The Microsoft website (www.microsoft.com), for instance, has thousands of pages about the fruits of the Gates empire. Each site has a 'home page' – it's the first page that's displayed when you visit the site. The home page is almost always stored in a file named 'index.html'. If you type in a website address without a specific web page, you'll see the home page. Visit 'http://www.bbc.co.uk' or 'http://www.bbc.co.uk/index.html' and you'll see the same opening page.

Sometimes, you'll see an address like 'http://www.compuserve.com/simon/'. This is an example of a small individual website located in an all-encompassing larger domain and it is totally different from 'http://www.compuserve.com/fred/'. These types of address are very common in smaller, enthusiast-run sites. Two of the biggest companies that will supply a free website for any enthusiast are GeoCities (http://www.geocities.com) and Tripod (http://www.tripod.com) – you'll see plenty of sites with these addresses as you surf or search the web.

> Remember just how important it is to make sure your computer and software are configured to protect your children from the obscene and antisocial material on the Internet. There are many different ways to block access to these sites – see Chapter 3, 'Net Worries', for full details.

Web addresses

Every website, page or image has its own unique address on the Internet. A website has a unique address called a 'domain name' – so the BBC's website (http://www.bbc.co.uk) has the domain name 'bbc.co.uk'. Each page on every website also has its own unique address, which is called its URL (uniform resource locator). A URL points to a particular web page, file, image or sound, whereas a domain name points to a site in general.

> Save typing effort – in every modern browser you don't need to type in the 'http://' prefix in front of a URL as it will automatically add it for you.

If you want to specify a particular web page on a website, you'll need to include the name of the file and the folder that contains the file. For example, if you want to see the latest news from the BBC, you could enter the URL 'http://www.bbc.co.uk/home/today/index.shtml'. Thankfully, it's very unusual to have to type in such a precise link – you'll normally find a page by clicking on a link embedded in another page.

What do all the letters and slashes mean?
You'll see plenty of different types of web address. Here's a guide to the various elements.

http:// the first part of any web address is 'http://' – it tells the browser you want to view a website.

https:// another indication (with the closed-padlock icon at the bottom of the window), that you're viewing a secure website.

www.bbc.co.uk the name of the computer that contains the pages for this site – called the domain name. Normally, computers that store websites start with 'www', but on some vast sites, you may see a web address like 'reg.bbc.co.uk', which indicates you are on a secondary machine, called 'reg' but still viewing the same domain name of 'bbc.co.uk'.

194.207.0.252 the number that uniquely identifies every domain name on the web.

index.html The name of the file that contains one web page.

Typing in the address '**http://www.bbc.co.uk**' will display the same site as the identical address '**http://194.207.0.252**'.

Web browsers

To view and surf web pages you'll need special software called a web browser. Its job is simply to decode the instructions stored in a web page file and display the formatted results on screen.

There are two main contenders in the browser market: Microsoft's Internet Explorer and Netscape's Navigator. Each company tries to introduce new technological trickery that will improve the web – and foil its rival. Both have leapfrogged each other over the years so now there's little difference between the two. And there's no price difference either – both are free (from **http://www.microsoft.com** and **http://www.netscape.com**), bundled with a new computer, or available to download, or on free CDs, and both run on PCs and Macs.

Net users who want to shun big corporations have several excellent smaller rivals to choose from including Opera (**http://www.operasoftware.com**). There are browsers for almost every type of computer and operating system; even if you have an old pre-Windows computer, you can still view web pages using the Arachne browser (**http://arachne.browser.org**).

There's just one other thing you need to know about browsers. The HTML language, which web pages are written in, is supposed to be a nice, easy standard. But because each browser manufacturer keeps trying to up the ante and improve on HTML, the different web browsers support different levels of HTML and its extensions.

The irritating truth is that if you visit the same website with two different browsers, you'll get a different look and layout. Some sites are designed to be best viewed with a Microsoft browser, others with Netscape's.

What's in a browser?

Install a web browser and you'll install a whole range of Internet software. Microsoft, Netscape and Opera all provide the basic ability to display web pages, but also provide an email program, newsgroup reader, chat program, an editor for web-page authoring and tools to make telephone calls over the Internet.

Using your web browser

Once you've signed up with an ISP and installed their software (see Chapter 2), you're ready to start surfing. When you run your web browser it should automatically start the dialler program that dials the access number and connects you to the Internet. It normally takes just under a minute to connect to the net – the dialler tells you what stage it's got to.

Once you are connected, the web browser automatically displays a 'home page'. This will probably be your ISP's main page, for example the Freeserve or Virgin Net page. You don't have to stick with the preassigned 'home page' – it's easy to change your web browser so that it displays your favourite sports page, shopping site or newspaper.

How to change your browser's home page

1   Start your web browser, connect to the Internet and visit your favourite site.

2   With the main page of the site displayed, select the Tools/Internet Options menu in IE or Edit/Preferences in Navigator.

A new dialog box is displayed; near the top there's a field with the site address of the current home page. Click on the button 'Use Current Page' to automatically insert the current site address.

Click on the OK button to confirm. Now, each time you start your browser, it displays your favourite page.

Navigating There are several different ways of moving (surfing) from one website or page to another.

Move to a new site or page by typing in the address in the address window in the top left corner.

Jump from one page to another by clicking on links in the page.

Move back through the previous pages that you visited in this session by clicking on the back arrow in the button bar.

Visiting a site Just under the menu bar in the top left-hand corner is the Address window where you type in the URL for the website you want to visit. Click in the window and type in the address of the site you want to visit – for example 'www.bbc.co.uk' for the BBC's excellent website. (You don't need to type in the initial http:// of an address – the browser fills this in for you.)

Once you have typed in the address, press Return and the web browser tries to find and display the page. If it cannot find the site or page, you'll see an error message; check you have typed the address in correctly and try again.

Surfing The main part of a web-browser window displays the web page. You'll see the text and layout defined according to the HTML instructions in the page. Hyperlinks normally appear on the page as underlined text. As you move your pointer over a link you'll see it change to a pointing-hand icon. Click once and you'll jump to a new page.

You can display several separate copies of the browser window by pressing Ctrl-N (or Apple-N on a Mac). Each window work independently, so you can view separate sites or pages in each use this tip to view share prices in one window while you brows sports results in another.

One extra tip that's particularly useful when using a search engin is to press down the Shift key when you click on a link in IE or right click on a link and select the 'Open in a new window' option i Navigator. This opens the new page in a new browser window – it an ideal way of keeping search results in one window while you'r checking out the site in another.

Bookmarking your favourite sites If you visit a site or page you'r likely to visit again, you can bookmark it: choose the Bookmark menu option in Netscape (or the Favorites menu option i Microsoft IE). Another way to do this is to press Ctrl-B unde Windows or Option-B on your Macintosh. It will store the site address, and its name, in a special list you access via a pull-dow menu. To go back to a bookmarked site, just click on the entry i the list.

As you start to create more bookmarks, you can organise you websites into different folders for different categories. To create folder in Netscape select the Communicator/Bookmarks/Ed Bookmarks menu option. From the new window that's displayed select the File/New Folder option. In Microsoft IE, choose th Favorites/Organize Favorites menu option and click on the Ne Folder button.

When you add a new bookmark, you may be asked if you want t subscribe to this site. This happens only if the site designer ha provided support for this advanced option. Choose 'yes' an you will be informed whenever the page changes. This is grea if you want to keep up to date with a company's news c software updates.

Security If you're about to type in any important personal or financial information at a website – such as your credit-card number when paying for shopping – make sure you are aware of security. The Internet was not designed to transfer private, personal information; if you send anything over the Internet, it is transferred in a plain, readable form.

The upshot of this is that someone else can tap your phone line, and read whatever you send or receive. Sounds awful, but in practice it's pretty hard to do and is usually not worth the bother from the hacker's point of view. If you want to send credit-card details and other personal information over the Internet, it's important that you don't do so in a form that can be intercepted. Secure websites were developed to provide a secure channel between your browser and the website.

When your browser has established a secure channel, a tiny closed-padlock icon is displayed in the status bar at the bottom of the browser window. All the new, current versions of web browsers support a security system called Secure Sockets Layer (SSL). If you have an older version of a browser or just want to check everything is working, visit the VeriSign site (http://www.verisign.com) and use the online test that tells you if your browser is SSL-compatible.

Don't type in your credit-card details or other personal information unless you see the closed-padlock icon in the bottom line of your web browser.

Printing pages You can print any page that you display. If the page uses frames for layout, you can print just one frame or the entire page. Microsoft Internet Explorer provides print options in the print window (choose File/Print menu) and will ask which frame of the page you want to display. To get something that looks just like the original on screen, choose the 'As Laid Out on Screen' option. In Netscape, the File/Print option changes to File/Print Frame – allowing you to choose and print one frame.

Controlling the browser

Running along the bottom of the browser window is the status line. In the left-hand corner of the Microsoft IE status line (or the right-hand corner of Netscape) is the full URL of the current page. If you type in a new address, the status line tells you what's happening as the browser tries to find and display the page you've requested.

Stopping an action Sometimes, the browser may seem to freeze or load very slowly. This is normally because the Internet is busy, or it cannot find a site – or the site is overloaded and taking a long time to reply. Time is precious, so stop the browser waiting for a reply by clicking on the Stop icon in the button bar at the top of the window.

Refresh a page Click the Refresh button in Microsoft IE (the Reload button in Netscape) in the button bar to reload and redisplay your current page. Why do this? If you're viewing a news page or page with share prices, clicking the Refresh button will display any updated information. Similarly, if the page freezes or looks odd, there may have been a temporary problem with the link. Click the Stop button, then the Refresh button to try again.

Dud technologies

Now and then, the Internet throws up some hopeless technology. Channels is one of them. The idea was to get the website to send you new information as it arrived. A kind of instant news update type of thing. Unfortunately, few companies could provide the content and users could just visit the home page for an update.

Cookies

Forget Rich Tea. A cookie is a scrap of information created by a website on your hard disk that lets the website store information

help it keep track of you. When you revisit the website, it reads
ne cookie, which tells it when you last visited, or what you did or
were interested in. For example, if you customise the Excite!
(www.excite.co.uk) or MSN (www.msn.co.uk) portal pages so that
ney display the weather in Manchester and the latest racing
esults, these choices are stored in a cookie.

enerally, there's nothing dangerous about cookies, but it can be
isconcerting to visit a site and be welcomed with a message that
ays, 'Back again? You were only here yesterday evening.' Most
tes use cookies only to keep track of your visits and your custom
ptions, giving them valuable marketing information that helps
em to tailor and improve their site. Only the geekiest sites use
ookies for silliness. Ignore them.

Controlling cookies

You can switch off support for cookies, but you'll lose out
on lots of neat features and shopping services. To switch
them off, change the security settings in your web browser:
for example, in Microsoft Internet Explorer, choose the
Tools/Internet Options menu, click on the Security page
tab and click on the Custom Level button. From the list,
scroll down till you see 'Cookies' and change 'Enable'
to 'Disable'.

---

aving information from the web

nything that's displayed on a web page can be saved on to your
omputer – except some types of video and music playback. Here's
ow to do it.

opying text Select the text you want to copy from the page by
cking and holding down the button while moving the mouse.
hen it's highlighted, press Ctrl-C to copy the text to the Clipboard
r Apple-C on a Mac). Switch to your word processor and press
rl-V (or Apple-V) to paste the text into any open file.

Saving an image Move the pointer over the image you want to save and click once. Select the File/Save Image As option from the main menu bar. Under Windows, move your pointer over the image then right-click to display the pop-up menu and choose the Save Image As option to store the image as a separate file on your hard disk.

Copying the code If you are developing your own website, you'll find it useful to see how the pros have pushed HTML to its limits to create their sites. Visit a site you particularly like and from the main menu bar select the View/Source option (in Internet Explorer) or View/Page Source (in Navigator); a new window pops up displaying the HTML source code for the page. If the page has been designed with frames (most advanced pages now use frames) move the pointer over the area of the page you want to investigate and again choose View/Source to see the code for this frame.

Saving a sound or video file Move the pointer over the hyperlink that leads to the sound or video file. Right-click over the link (this works only on a PC) and choose the Save Target As menu option.

Saving the location of a page Either create a new Bookmark or Favorite entry in your web browser or click anywhere on the page then drag it on to your desktop. You'll create an icon with a shortcut to the site's address.

Downloading files
The Internet has millions of files that you can pull off a website and store on your hard disk. The files include updates to your software application, images, sound, databases or even full programs. There are two ways to download files to your computer. Most large commercial sites display details of the file together with a hyperlink – click on the link and your browser automatically starts to download the selected file. The browser displays a dialog box giving you the option to save the file on to your hard disk or run the

file. Select the Save option and the file will start to be transferred to your computer.

Handling compressed files

Most files are compressed before they are stored on the Internet ready for you to download – this saves download time. If you've just bought a new application, it's probably packaged up as a self-extracting file: double-click on the file and it expands itself, then installs itself.

On a Macintosh, many compressed file names end 'SEA' – click on them and they will decompress themselves automatically without any extra software. Alternative popular, compressed Mac file formats are HQX and SIT. For PC files, most compressed filenames end with the letters 'ZIP', and you'll need an unzip utility to decompress the program. The most popular is WinZip (http://www.winzip.com), or you'll find alternatives at Filez (http://www.filez.com) or CNET (http://www.cnet.com).

FTP servers If a computer is dedicated to storing files ready for you to download, it's called an FTP server. A good example is ftp://www.microsoft.com, which stores thousands of its programs, update files and demonstration software. To access an FTP server you can use specialist software (that's also vital if you want to publish a website or do seriously advanced net stuff). Luckily for the rest of us, web browsers can connect to an FTP server just fine.

Many FTP servers ask you to type in a user name and password before you can view the list of files. Most allow guests to enter and download files by logging in as an anonymous user. Type in 'anonymous' as a user ID and your email address as the password, and you should see a listing of the folders and files available to download.

For users who plan to do a lot of file transfers, or visit academic sites (who mostly still use FTP servers with anonymous login), you'll find life easier with an FTP client program. These are all shareware or freeware. Visit CNET (http://www.cnet.com) or Filez (http://www.filez.com) and search for FTP – you'll get a list of the latest versions of the top clients. Click on a link and let your browser download the program.

If you download any file from the Internet, make sure that you check that it is clear of viruses before you open or run it. Use a special antivirus program such as McAfee (http://www.mcafee.com) or Norton AntiVirus (http://www.symantec.com).

Music and movies

Music and video are played on the coolest sites, providing a complete multimedia experience. Visit the All-Music Guide (http://www.allmusic.com), for example, and you'll be able to listen to music clips and watch video segments of thousands of bands. To experience either type of clip, your web browser needs to support the special file and transfer format used by the site. This being the confusing world of the Internet, there are, naturally, several competing standards.

The newest web browsers include support for most standard ways of transferring music, video and animation over the web, so just sit back and enjoy. If your browser doesn't support the standard, you'll see a warning message that asks if you want to download a special software program – called a plug-in – that works with your web browser to play back the music or video.

The download and installation are automatic and your newly enhanced browser will be able to play back multimedia clips stored in this particular format.

Play that funky music

There are two ways of making music available on the net. One is to store the music in a digital computer file that can be downloaded and played on a computer (this technique is used by MP3 and WAV files). Another is to play the music back, live, over the Internet connection (as with Real).

You can download dedicated playback software at:

http://www.mp3.com
http://mp3.lycos.com
http://www.mp3.dk
http://www.rioport.com
http://www.real.com
http://www.winamp.com

Browsing offline

It is relatively easy to view web pages even when you're not connected to the Internet. The first method uses the temporary files that your web browser stores on your hard disk as you browse. First, you'll need to visit the web pages you want to read and make sure they have downloaded on to your computer (you'll see the word 'Done' displayed in the bottom status bar when the page has finished downloading and is temporarily stored on your hard disk). Zip from one page to the next and they'll each be stored on your disk.

Next, select the File/Work Offline option in IE or the File/Go Offline menu option in Navigator and your browser will disconnect from the Internet. Now type in the URL of a page you've visited recently and the browser should be able to display it. (The temporary files are stored for only a certain amount of time, so it may not be there.) If you try to view a page that's no longer in the temporary store (called the cache), the browser will attempt to dial up and connect to the Internet.

The second method is to use a specialist utility program that saunters up to a website and downloads the whole lot on to your hard disk. This was a fine idea when websites had just a few dozen pages, but try this on the CNN or BBC site and you'll wait around for days as the thousands of individual pages are downloaded. Once you have downloaded the site on to your drive, you can browse it as if you were online. The best known of these utilities are Teleport (http://www.tenmax.com), UnMozify (http://www.evolve.co.uk), Insite (http://www.engr.orst.edu/~schonfal/inst.htm) and WebWhacker (http://www.webwhacker.com).

//ADDRESS BOOK

Web browsers

The free software you need to view and surf web pages.

Microsoft	http://www.microsoft.com
Netscape	http://www.netscape.com
Opera	http://www.opera.com
ICAB	http://www.icab.de
Lynx	http://lynx.browser.org
SurfMonkey	http://www.surfmonkey.com
Neoplanet	http://www.neoplanet.com

5//FINDING THINGS OUT

The Internet contains everything you could ever want to know, and quite a lot of things that you don't. But how do you find what you want? With over 50 million web pages out there, you'll need plenty of help to hunt out a site that's relevant.

We've put some of the most useful sites in this book, but there's no way we can cover the enormous range of information there is on the net. Fortunately, there are several ways to find information and interesting sites anywhere on the Internet.

Start searching

To help you find a web page that contains things that you want to know, you'll need to use a special search website. These are websites whose sole job is to provide an index of website addresses listed according to key words and descriptions in the original page. Type in a word or phrase and you'll see a list of websites and their addresses that match your search request. As usual, the Internet provides plenty of choice with hundreds of different sites that help you find other relevant sites and information. These search sites arrange their indexes in one of two different ways.

Search engine This type of site tries to include every single scrap of information that's on every site in the web. These are vast and good for a general query – but you'll get thousands of answers. Some of the biggest include AltaVista, Lycos and Excite!

Search directory This type of site limits itself to just a few hundred thousand links. Each one is normally checked by a real person before being added – some directories even mark the entries. The best known is Yahoo! and its child-friendly spin-off Yahooligans!

For the gentle stroll about the web, or to find every site about a subject, try a general search engine like AltaVista or Excite! These tame monsters let you search their vast databases, which list almost every web page that's published. But be careful: a simple search can swamp you with hundreds of thousands of unsorted matching results – and with no guarantee that the material's suitable for children.

For a more structured approach, try a directory. The top directory is Yahoo!. The big Y and its lesser rivals list a select half-million or so sites under specific categories, rather like the Yellow Pages telephone directory. You can either search the directory, or browse through a particular category.

One problem with all of the search directories and even the biggest, most comprehensive search engines is that they cannot possibly index all the websites on the Internet. To keep up with the flood of new information, the search engines would have to try to visit and index hundreds of thousands of new web pages every day, but their software, their disk capacity and the Internet itself are not fast enough to cope with this. Instead, you can be sure that, for the millions of sites that are listed, there are many times as many undiscovered.

Recent reports have suggested that out of the near-billion web pages that are on the web, search engines are indexing under 20 per cent of this total.

Metasearching and search assistants Climbing on to our soapbox, we think the best way to search the web is to use a metasearch tool. Don't bother hiking from one search engine to another: let the metasearcher do the legwork for you. Just visit the metasearch site, type in your question and it will automatically submit the question to all the main search engines and directories, then filter the answers for relevance and present you with a manageable list of answers.

Sites like Google, All-in-One and Metacrawler are a great way to benefit from the range of search engines without the bother of visiting each one.

Top metasearch sites

All-in-One	http://www.allonesearch.com
Go2Net: MetaCrawler	http://www.metacrawler.com
DogPile	http://www.dogpile.com
Google	http://www.google.com
Savvy Search	http://www.savvysearch.com

Search assistants sit somewhere between a metasearcher and a directory – the best known is AskJeeves (http://www.askjeeves.com) and its child-friendly AskJeevesForKids (http://www.ajkids.com). Either site lets you type in a question in plain English; it then lists all the possible answers that it knows about – or the sites it thinks may help you with an answer. It'll often come up with wild oddball answers, but generally, it's a good place to start looking if you want to know the answer to a simple question – like the capital of Finland or the films that starred Sinatra.

Child-friendly searching

The standard range of search engines and directories cover everything on the Internet – and much of the content is going to be unsuitable for children. Try typing in the word 'sex' or 'nudes' into a search engine and view the millions of matching sites. Even an innocent search for information on rubber, videos or Bangkok could turn up some highly unsuitable information.

There are plenty of ways of limiting the search results so that these pornographic sites don't appear. The best way is to use special software that filters out any obscene words or sites and limits what your kids can type in and view. See page 25 for details on setting up your computer with this filtering software.

If children are researching homework or just finding interesting sites, a search engine or directory is essential. To provide for this, most of the major search engines and directories include family-friendly features. The bigger search engines, such as AltaVista, include controls to help filter out results with an adult theme – but they are not foolproof: a child can visit another search engine, type in an address directly or simply switch off the feature.

Given the natural curiosity of children, it's better to point them to a search engine that doesn't contain any unsuitable material at all. The best known (and best all round) is Yahooligans! (http://www.yahooligans.com), with AskJeevesForKids (http://www.ajkids.com) a close second. Both provide a directory of hundreds of thousands of child-friendly sites that parents can be confident won't lead to obscene pages. The contents of this and other family-friendly directories have been checked for content by a real human editor and are safe for children to browse for themselves.

The directories normally include mini-reviews and ratings and group the sites into categories for hobbies, sports and so on.

How to search

Start your browser and type in the address of your favourite search engine – take a tour of the search engines listed in the Address Book at the end of this chapter and choose the one you like best.

Now that you're at a search site, you'll see that pride of place on the page goes to the search entry field. Type in the keywords you want to search with (some sites let you type in a question) and click the button beside the field or hit Return. Your query is now sent to another computer that contains the search engine's software. It zips through its index of millions of websites and displays a list of matching sites, all within a second or two. The search results are usually listed by relevance: the site that best matches your question or keywords is displayed first. Each result will display the name of the page, its address and a short description (extracted from the page itself).

Click on the address and you'll jump immediately to the page – if the address is still working. One of the problems of this type of general search is that websites are always changing. The information in the search engine index is always a little out of date and you'll probably find many of the search-result links don't work simply because the site has closed or moved. (See page 60 for more details on how to solve this problem.)

A quick way of adding a little zing to your web searches is to use a built-in feature of the new versions of Microsoft Internet Explorer v5 and Netscape Navigator. When you've found a site you like, click on the 'Show Related Sites' menu in IE or the What's Related button in Navigator toolbar; the screen splits and you'll see a list of sites covering similar subjects.

Fine-tune your search

It's a doddle to carry out a simple search – just type in your question. But this could easily result in thousands of results – you need to fine-tune your search question so that you weed out the irrelevant sites. Progress to the status of savvy-searcher by using the power tricks described in the box – these are part of all search engines.

As you sift through your results, you'll soon realise that the engine is searching for all your words in any order. The next step to power status is to match an exact expression. To do this, enclose the expression in quote marks. For example, if you want to find a dairy that still makes original Devon cream, type in 'Devon cream', with the quote marks. If you don't, you'll probably see sites that list the cream of Devon fishing, and restaurants in Leeds offering Devon plaice with cream of mushroom sauce.

Power search techniques

If you want to use any other search site, you'll have to use a rather techie notation for your queries. Almost all the search engines, including Yahoo! and Excite!, let you refine your query using the '+' and '-' symbols. If you put a '+' sign in front of a word, it means the word must be matched. And the '-' works in just the opposite way. For example, to find sites about Belgian micro-breweries specialising in flavoured ales you would enter +Belgium +micro +brewery + flavoured +beer -lager.

The second way to power search is to use Boolean operators – named after the English mathematician George Boole (1815–64), who invented a way of using mathematics to express logic. These are the simple words 'AND', 'OR' and 'NOT', which you can insert between search terms. For example, if you want to find sites about Teletubbies jigsaw puzzles, you would enter Teletubbies AND jigsaw. Similarly, to find the sites dedicated to Tinky Winky, and not to Po, you would enter Teletubbies AND Tinky Winky NOT Po.

If you're trying to search for a particular subject, look at the directory sites in the Starting Points of each section of our subject directory. There's less dross than with a general search engine and they're more interesting.

Dead addresses

Websites get launched, change name and get redesigned all the time. This makes it rather tricky for the search engines to keep track of what's going on and as a result many of their suggestions are likely to be pages that no longer exist. You'll see the problem when you start to search – many of the links thrown up just won't work when you click on them. You'll get the classic warning, 'Error, page not found', or 'Error 404', which tells you the address cannot be found.

With some ingenuity and lateral thinking, you can still track down the site. One of the most common problems is that the site's designer changes the names of the individual pages within the site – the site itself is probably still available, but the page registered at the search engine no longer matches.

y editing the address to delete chunks from the address after
ach '/' symbol. Click on the address field at the top of your
rowser and use the arrow and delete keys to edit the address.
'ess Return to see if this works and, if not, continue editing.

pecialist search software

stead of using a search engine on the Internet, you could use a
pecial software package that runs on your PC. They all cost money
nd all effectively do the same as a metasearcher. Load the
oftware on to your computer (it normally appears as a new button
n your web browser's toolbar) and type in your query – as
omplicated as you like. The software zips around the Internet to
I the search engines to find sites that'll match your answer.

he more sophisticated versions will even answer questions from
neir own database. Many of these tools are now converting
to web-based search sites, but there are still a few separate
rograms that work with your browser. Three of the better-known
re: CyberPilot (http://www.netcarta.com), Poke (http://www.
ebprowler.com) and the elderly WebCompass (http://www.
rmantec.com).

A new system called RealNames is being promoted as the alternative to
all those confusing web addresses. Instead of typing in a company's
address, just type in their company name. For example, if you want to
find the site for the London *Evening Standard* newspaper, you could use
a search engine or find the address (http://www.thisislondon.co.uk) or
just type in the RealNames keywords 'Evening Standard'. The system is
part of Internet Explorer 5, or you can download the special software
(from http://www.realnames.com) that works with any browser.

---

ortals

Vhen a website decides to rule the world, it calls itself a portal.
nese vast sites want to be your friend and to be the starting
oint and one-stop solution to all your browsing needs. You'll find

weather, news, sport, finance and a whole load of trendy inf
sources that embellish the basic search engine. The compan
behind any portal is trying to maintain a large, regular group c
visitors who want to keep coming back. Once they have th
audience, they can sell advertising space and provide their ow
shops and special offers.

All of the main search engines have evolved into portal sites, bu
Yahooligans! (http://www.yahooligans.com) is the best for kid:
whereas Excite! (http://www.excite.co.uk) and MSN (http://www
msn.co.uk) have done the most to make grown-ups feel at home.

//ADDRESS BOOK

Family-friendly Sites

AskJeevesForKids   http://www.ajkids.con
When you get asked something you don't know, tell your kids t
ask this impeccably polite character. Fantastically easy to use – yo
ask, it answers.

Berit's Best Sites   http://db.cochran.com
for Children   li_toc:theoPage.d
Safe and fun sites for kids, rated to help parents.

Bonus.com   http://www.bonus.con
Vast clubhouse of a site, which includes reviews of masses of site:
When you visit, your browser will disappear and be replaced by th
restrictive but child-friendly browser, NetScooter (click on the Clos
button to get back to your normal browser).

EdViews   http://www.edview.com
Listings of over 25,000 teacher-approved websites that are safe c
educational for children to visit.

Great Sites   http://www.ala.org/parentspage/greatsites
Hundreds of safe, friendly sites from the American Librar
Association – so there's plenty on books and reading.

IPL Youth Division   http://www.ipl.org/youth/
Uninspiring name, but a good place to start browsing the directory
of friendly sites, supplied by the Internet Public Library.

KidsClick!   http://sunsite.berkeley.edu/KidsClick!/
Thousands of children-friendly sites sorted, rated and reviewed
neatly into categories by a team of librarians.

Kids Online   http://www.aaa.com.au/Kids_Radio.shtml
More sites than you can shake a rattle at.

Kidz Guide to the Internet   http://www.4kidz.com/
Good directory of friendly, safe and useful sites.

Route 6-16   http://www.cyberpatrol.com/616/default.htm
Vast collection of sites rated safe for six- to sixteen-year-olds – the
list that's used by the Cyber Patrol software to prevent your
children viewing unsuitable material.

SafeSurf Kid's Wave   http://www.safesurf.com/kidswave.htm
Good selection of interesting sites for children to visit.

Surfing the net with Kids   http://www.surfnetkids.com/
A few selected sites rated and reviewed by the host, an American
newspaper columnist.

The Family Grapevine   http://www.thegrapevine.co.uk
Directory of national telephone helplines and local directories for
different parts of the UK.

Tristan and Tiffany   http://www.tnt.to/
Cool sites, as recommended by two kids, Tristan and Tiffany.

Yahooligans!   http://www.yahooligans.com
Ditch the grown-up stuff – it's strictly cartoons, homework and fun
at this niche site from Yahoo!

Finding Sites Designed by Kids

There are thousands of great sites devised and designed by smart kids. Try these directories to find 'em.

Kids' Space Connection   http://www.ks-connection.org/
Yahooligans!   http://www.yahooligans.com/

General-Purpose Search Engines

These provide a vast index of almost every website on the Internet. Try these sites if you want to find something obscure. You can type in a search word and you'll get hundreds – often hundreds or thousands – of matching sites. Top sites like AltaVista and Excite! let you type in a normal English sentence. If you're really serious about your searching, check out the 'read me' sections at the search engine site for full details of how to get the best out of it.

All The Web   http://www.alltheweb.com
Just about the biggest engine around, but it can be overwhelming

AltaVista   http://www.altavista.com
Boasts just about the biggest index on the web.

Euroseek   http://www.euroseek.net
Europhiles head for this multilingual, multicountry search engine.

Excite!   http://www.excite.co.uk
Another mammoth index that includes a directory.

G.O.D.   http://www.god.co.uk
British and proud of it!

HotBot   http://www.hotbot.com
Just about the friendliest engine on the web, but a bit US-biased.

Infoseek   http://www.infoseek.co.uk
The best all-round player.

Lycos   http://www.lycos.co.uk
The granddaddy of search engines; great for MP3 music samples.

WebCrawler   http://www.webcrawler.com

If it's out there, you'll probably find it in here.

Directories

When you've recovered from the million matches to your simple AltaVista query about 'golf balls', you may wonder how to avoid the dross that clogs up most search results. Directories use advanced technology (humans) who visit each site and take a look before adding it to their listings. The listings are organised into categories, so you can browse all the plumbers or do a general search for plumbing. You're unlikely to stumble across a rare gem, but you will find what you're looking for.

About   http://www.about.com

One person is assigned to each category. Very friendly, very cosy.

LookSmart   http://www.looksmart.co.uk

Easier to navigate than Yahoo! and each site gets a comment.

Magellan   http://www.mckinley.com

Each site in the index gets a review and a star rating.

Northern Light   http://www.northernlight.com

Vast, fast and accurate.

Scoot   http://www.scoot.co.uk

Brilliant collection of local information from around the UK.

UKPlus   http://www.ukplus.com

Find UK-specific sites in a hurry.

Yahoo!   http://www.yahoo.co.uk

Dominates the web; contains only a half-million or so sites, but these are clearly organised. Also provides a vast range of extra goodies – you might never want to leave.

Yell   http://www.yell.co.uk

Not the easiest to use, but the biggest in the UK.

Metasearchers

Silly name for a good idea. These chaps will do all the hard work for you and submit your query to all the search engines and directories in one go – then return the top hits. A perfect way to turbo-boost your searches.

All-in-One   http://www.albany.net/allinone
Does all the digging for you, and at high speed.

AskJeeves   http://www.askjeeves.com
Great service and generally comes up trumps.

DogPile   http://www.dogpile.com
Hardly elegant sophistication, but great for specific searches.

Google   http://www.google.com
Clear, fast and effective – it's particularly good at weeding out irrelevant results.

Go2Net: MetaCrawler   http://www.metacrawler.com
Returns a manageable few results from the major search engines.

Savvy Search   http://www.savvysearch.com
Searches a couple of dozen of the top search engines.

Something specific

Specific bits of the Internet each have their own search engines. Most of the big search engines (like Yahoo! and Excite!) let you search the nonweb parts of the Internet (newsgroups, email, mailing lists) – or you can use one of the subject-specific search engines that we've listed at the end of each relevant chapter (for example, to find email addresses, see page 78 and to find the cheapest place to shop, see page 214).

6//ELECTRONIC MAIL

Electronic mail (email) is still one of the best reasons to get on the Internet. It's a fast, cheap and very convenient way of sending messages and files to any other user. To keep in touch with your pals or distant relatives, without transatlantic phone bills, send them an email.

You can write your emails any time – you don't need to be online running up the phone bill. The best idea is to write all your messages offline, connect to send these and receive any new mail, then disconnect and read your new messages.

And if you have one of the newer WAP (wireless application protocol) mobile telephones, you can send and receive email to anyone from anywhere.

Family email

If you're bringing your family online, make absolutely sure that your ISP gives you more than one email address. Most companies, including AOL, Freeserve and Virgin Net, give you five separate email addresses – so each person in the family can have their own, totally independent email address. For example, if Mr Smith registers with Freeserve, his email address could be 'simon@smith_family.freeserve.co.uk'. He can also set up 'francesca@smith_family.freeserve.co.uk' and his son 'nicholas@smith_family.freeserve.co.uk'.

In order to read your email messages, you can either configure your email software to retrieve all the mail for the 'smith_family' accounts or, with sophisticated email software, you can set up a separate identity for each member of the family. If you follow your ISP's directions, you'll probably set up the former – in which the mail for the entire family is retrieved in one go.

To help organise your family's incoming messages you could create a folder for each person and create a rule that automatically moves messages into the correct folder – according to the person's name. (See later in this chapter for how to do this.) If you're using Microsoft Outlook or Qualcomm Eudora, or if you have installed the multiple 'Users' feature of Windows, then each member of the family can have their own, totally separate mail box.

AOL members use customised software provided by AOL, which manages the separate email accounts for you – each member of the family can have their own account and email address right from the start.

Email standards
The standard type of email account used by most people is provided by their Internet Service Provider. When you sign up, your computer is configured to send and receive mail messages via a central server computer located at your ISP – called the post office. This server temporarily stores your incoming messages till you go online and collect and download them to your computer. If you send a message, your email software passes it to the server, which in turn sends it over the Internet to its destination.

Email is normally sent using a system called SMTP (simple mail-transfer protocol) and received using a different system called POP3 (post office protocol-3). Almost all email programs support this SMTP/POP3 mix of standards. Most decent ISPs will provide preconfigured software in their starter packs.

Changes are on the way to make your email account more flexible. At the moment, it's hard to check and send your email when you're away from your PC (unless you use a web-based account like HotMail or Yahoo! Mail). To solve this, a new standard called IMAP (Internet Message-Access Protocol) is being introduced. At the moment, it's still mostly used by large companies but it will reach you within a year or two.

Children and email

They're going to want to exchange emails with their friends, but you would probably prefer your children not to receive unwanted mail and you would certainly want to prevent hate mail or harassment.

There are, thankfully, lots of ways to protect your children when they use email. Look to Chapter 3 for full details.

Your first email

You can reassure yourself how easy it is to use email by sending us your first email. It's a quick way to check that you understand the simple steps for sending a message – and that you have correctly configured your email software. We'll reply in a few seconds, if you've got it right. Here's what to do:

1 Start your email program and move the pointer to the 'To' address box, click to select and type in the email address of our testing system – 'test@virgin-pub.co.uk'.

2 Move to the 'Subject' field, click to select and type in 'testing'.

3 Move to the main part of the message window and type a quick 'hello' as the main message – or even tell us what you think of our book.

4 Click the Send button. Now click on the Send/Receive icon (in Microsoft) or the Get Msg icon (in Netscape) to connect to the Internet and send the message.

5 Once the message has been sent, wait for around twenty or thirty seconds and click on Send/Receive button a second time. Our automatic reply will be delivered – click on it to read it. If you don't get the message, wait a little longer, then click on Send/Receive again.

//TYPES OF ACCOUNT

Email via your ISP Chances are, you are probably using a standard dial-up account from an ISP to send and receive your email. You may have a whole range of extra email features that you didn't know existed. The most popular, provided by lots of ISPs to paying customers, gives you several different email addresses (or 'POP3 accounts'). Use this feature to give everyone in your family their own email address.

Your email is temporarily stored on the ISP's server until you ask your email program to collect it and store it on your computer. You'll need a special email program to send and receive messages, but these are now supplied as part of the suite of software that comes with your web browser: Microsoft includes Outlook Express and Netscape includes Communicator. Alternatively, you can use a third-party email program such as Eudora (http://www.qualcomm.com) or Pegasus (http://www.pegasus-usa.net).

Free email Plenty of companies want to give you a free email account. They pay for the costs with advertising – either on their website or sent as messages to your new account. These email accounts are generally web-based: everything is done via a website. You won't get dial-up access to the Internet, just a new email address. You don't use a special email program to manage your messages; you'll need an Internet account from an ISP to access the net, then you can send, receive and check your email using any basic web browser.

If you have signed up for free email-only account (from HotMail, Yahoo! Mail or any of the hundreds of other companies), you are using this type of system. It works in a very different way from a POP3 account that's supplied by your ISP, but you can still send and receive messages to and from any other user on the Internet. The problem with this type of email account is that it can be slow to access, you can't write or read messages offline and you can get a lot of commercials in your in-tray.

However, you can take advantage of the freebies. You don't need to be limited to just one free email address: you can sign up for as many accounts as you want. It's a good way of providing separate email accounts for everyone in the family or for separate business and personal email addresses.

Many of the large children-friendly sites (such as Headbone, ShooZoo and Zeeks) let kids set up their own web-based email addresses. It's a good way to provide children with some independence within a controlled, safe environment; they'll need an account with an ISP and web browser to send or receive mail.

Reduce time online

If you have a standard POP3 email account (supplied by your ISP), write your messages offline, and then dial up and connect to the Internet to send all the messages in one go. While you're offline, new messages are stored in the OutBox folder. New messages are stored in the InBox folder until you read them – unless you have automatically routed them to a folder by a special rule.

Addressing an email

Email addresses are easy to mistype. Get one full stop or underscore wrong, and the message won't reach its destination. Unlike your friendly local postman who knows that Mrs Jones lives at number 14, not 41, email doesn't leave any margin for error.

An email address is made up of two parts. In the middle is an '@' symbol (pronounced 'at'), which divides the two parts. On the right is the address of the local server that handles the mail for this person. On the left is the person's user name on this server. For example, 'fred_bloggs@virgin-pub.co.uk' identifies a user called 'Fred Bloggs' who uses the domain 'virgin-pub.co.uk' (this domain could be his ISP or his company).

Address books Don't bother typing in addresses each time you want to send mail to your friends. Instead, use the address-book feature that's part of every mail program. To open the Address Book in Microsoft Outlook, use the Tools/Address Book menu option; in Netscape Navigator use Communicator/Address Book.

A feature of many email programs – like Outlook, Eudora and Communicator – is called autocomplete addressing. The program keeps track of the addresses you've used in the past; as you start to type in an address, the program automatically completes the address for you.

If you want to be sure someone has read your message, select the 'Confirm Read' option when you create it. When the recipient opens the message, you should get an automatic receipt to inform you that your message has been read. However, this doesn't always work.

Wrong address? Send a message to an email address that doesn't exist, and it will come swinging straight back. This is called a bounce and lets you know within a few minutes that the message could not be delivered. In most cases, the bounced message will also contain extra information that tells you what went wrong – the user name may not be recognised by the server or perhaps the server is down (being repaired) at that moment. Either way, check you have the right address, then try again.

There's no complete, central directory of email addresses to help you find someone's address. You've got three options: ask them, visit their company's website to see if there's a contact list or search one of the (rather limited) directories of addresses that do exist (such as Four11 at http://www.four11.com).

Multiple addresses There are plenty of times that you may want to send a message to more than one person at a time. If you organise a club or team, you can keep everyone up to date by setting up a mailing list or group of contacts. This is a feature of your email program's address book.

If you want to send your message to just a few people, use these extra sections at the top of the screen when you create it.

To: Type in the address of the person for whom your message is intended. You can list several addresses, separated by a comma or semicolon or space.

CC: (carbon copy) Type in the address of another person who should see a copy of this message. The person in the 'To:' field will know who else has seen the message.

BCC: (blind carbon copy) If you type in an address here, they'll receive a copy of the message, but the person in the 'To:' field won't be able to tell.

If you receive a message that was sent to a list of people using the CC feature, be careful when you reply to the message. You may mean to send it to the originator, but it could easily go to all the members on the list. Your email program should warn you if you're about to make this mistake.

Email etiquette

Assuming that in your pre-email days you didn't go around writing rude letters to strangers, you'll find the basic rules of email etiquette easy as pie. For a start, it's always nice to reply immediately to someone – even if it's just a quick acknowledgement that you received their message and are now dealing with it.

For some reason, people feel it's acceptable to ignore the usual rules that govern decency and decorum when they turn to an email. If you want to gossip about a friend, don't do it via email – it's too easy to forward, and someone can always keep a copy to hold against you. And, if you're writing a letter in a professional capacity, keep it professional.

Next, don't write emails in capital letters. On the Internet, this is how people shout – and no one likes SHOUTING. If you need a little help with your spelling, don't forget that there's a spell-checker built into most email programs.

See page 92 for a list of abbreviations commonly used in email.

Adding colour to a message Most email programs – such as Outlook and Messenger – let you format your message just like a word-processor document. You can change the fonts or colour, or even add images (such as your signature). This can look great, but many net users still work with email software that can read only plain, unformatted text. So, over the years, some common conventions have developed to replace underlining and bold in an email message.

To add emphasis to a word, surround it with '*' as in 'It made me *very* angry'. To describe an action or expression, use '<' and '>', as in 'I thought it was a great idea <sarcastic grin>'. Lastly, you can add expressions to your mail – or newsgroup postings – using what are known as smileys. Don't use them too often, but they work well in small doses. Here's what smileys mean (but you may need to tilt your head to the left a bit):

> :-) happy

> ;-) normally means winking and joking

> :-(sad

> :-o amazed

Sending files by email

You're not limited to plain text (letters) when sending email. You can attach any type of file – photos, databases, spreadsheets, music or video clips – to your email. It's free, quick and convenient. Unfortunately, this is also a good way to distribute pornography, filthy jokes or tasteless pictures. Most of the specialist software programs (including AOL's Parental Controls) allow you to prevent some members of the family from viewing or sending attachments.

To send a file, click on the paperclip icon in Microsoft Outlook (in Netscape, click on the paperclip icon, then choose the File option from the drop-down menu). You'll see a list of files on your computer: move to the folder and select the file you want to send.

Sending to fax, pager or telephone

Emails don't just go from computer to computer. You can turn your email into a fax message, or redirect it to a pager or even use email to send a text message to a mobile phone.

To send an email message to a fax machine, use one of the clever email-to-fax gateways; some are free, others will charge you for the privilege. Have a look at the gaudy Zipfax site (http://www.zipfax.com) or the simple Oxford University site (http://info.ox.ac.uk/fax/).

The latest mobile phones can access the Internet directly using WAP (Wireless Application Protocol) – find out more at www.wapforum.org

Although the main mobile-phone providers let you send text messages between phones, it's a different matter when it's web-to-phone. They're all trial systems, but, at the time of going to press, only Orange (http://www.orange.co.uk) seems to provide a consistent service, with Vodafone promising to offer the service soon.

Organise your email

Don't let all your email messages collect in one vast heap. Use folders and rules to organise messages into a model of neat, well-ordered efficiency. Every email program lets you create folders within the main InBox; you can drag and drop messages into folders to organise them or use rules to move messages automatically. If the whole family's sharing a single email address, you could use rules to move messages automatically to each member's folder, or you can use it to separate mail from friends, with messages from work colleagues.

Creating rules

Use rules to move and organise your email automatically (Microsoft calls this feature Message Rules, other programs call it rules or a filter). Rules are part of all good email programs and work in the background to scan new messages then organise them according to key words. Rules look for a word or term in a message – you could devise a simple rule that moves any message with 'football fixture' in the 'Subject' field into a folder called 'Priority'.

Mailing lists

Mailing lists let you share messages with all the other subscribers in the list. They are a simple and effective way to keep up to date with a special interest or with peer groups or colleagues. Everything is done through your normal email program. When you want to post a message to the group, send it to the list's management email address; this then distributes your message to everyone else on the list.

There are over 90,000 specialist mailing lists that let you join and discuss everything from car spares to music (such as a list to discuss the Chemical Brothers) – though the academic topics still dominate.

How do I find a suitable list? Finding a mailing list is easy. Most of the search engines on the web have a good database of lists, but it's better to visit one of the specialist mailing-list sites such as Liszt (http://www.liszt.com). Search for a subject and you'll get a range of lists available. Most have mini-descriptions and instructions on how to subscribe.

Problems with email

Fed up with junk mail? It doesn't stop with email, unfortunately. Unsolicited email is called spam; a company can send out millions of commercial messages to email addresses bought from a list merchant. Many Internet providers now subscribe to a central data-base that lists all the sources of spam and so blocks unwanted email.

Viruses Worse than spam are viruses spread by email (often called mail-bombs). When you open an email program with an infected file attached, it automatically spreads the virus to your computer or could even delete or damage files on your hard disk. Some viruses are specially written to attack your email software rather than any other files on your computer.

Watch out for messages that are called something like 'Virus warning' or 'Free money' – they are often the reverse and could contain a virus.

Another problem is viruses built into Microsoft Word documents as a macro (a series of commands that control Word). The latest versions of Word will warn you if you are about to open a document that contains a macro (in which case, it's safest to choose the 'disable macro' option, which will disable the virus).

To avoid being hit by virus attacks or mail-bombs, don't open mail with attachments unless you know the person who sent them and you have used special virus scanner software to detect any viruses. Two of the most popular detection programs are McAfee (http://www.mcafee.com) and Norton AntiVirus (http://www.symantec.com). These programs work in the background and will check any new mail messages as they arrive and warn you if they contain a virus. Because hackers are always developing new strains of virus, you'll need to download update files frequently for the antivirus software to make sure it can spot all the latest viruses.

ADDRESS BOOK

Email Software

Your web browser already has an email program as part of the bundle, and there's often little reason to change. However, if you really want to upgrade, then try these dedicated email packages that have lots of new features.

Outlook	http://www.microsoft.com
Eudora	http://www.qualcomm.com
Pegasus	http://www.pegasus.usa.net

Free Email Accounts for Everyone

Bigfoot	http://www.bigfoot.com
Excite!	http://www.excite.com
Hotmail	http://www.hotmail.com
RocketMail	http://www.rocketmail.com
Yahoo!	http://www.yahoo.com

Free Email Accounts for Kids

Headbone Zone	http://www.headbone.com
ShooZoo	http://www.shoozoo.com
Zeeks.com	http://www.zeeks.com

Finding an Address

There's no complete directory yet, but you can try looking up a name in the following directories of some people's addresses.

AltaVista	http://www.altavista.com
BigFoot	http://www.bigfoot.com
Excite	http://www.excite.com
Four11	http://www.four11.com
Who Where	http://www.whowhere.com
PeopleSite	http://www.peoplesite.com

Finding a Mailing List

Catalist	www.lsoft.com/lists/listref.htm
Liszt	www.liszt.com
Tile.net	www.tile.net

7//DISCUSSION AND CHAT

To many users, the Internet means the web – glossy pictures, clever design and lots of information. But for a net-head, the real heart of the Internet lies in newsgroups and chat. But beware! If you're setting up your computer for your children, be very careful before you allow them access to either.

In the real world, news means newspapers, breaking stories and reports, but on the net it means newsgroups. To get the full effect of free speech, take a tour of the Internet's newsgroups – collectively called Usenet. Very little has changed in the way you access newsgroups since the Internet was first developed. It's as simple as email and just about as powerful. There are over 60,000 different discussion groups that together provide the most active, obnoxious and, for children, potentially one of the most dangerous parts of the whole Internet experience – as people use chat as a medium to say whatever they want.

Internet chat is like an instant email: whatever you type in is seen by the other users in the 'room'. Chatting sounds harmless enough, but it can easily get out of control. Your children could easily give out more personal information than intended, they don't know who they're chatting to and there are now cases of some nutters stalking or harassing kids via chat.

Newsgroups and children

Newsgroups can be great fun when you're chatting about sport, music or hobbies, but they can be full of crude, obscene language and are not the place for young children. However, you might want to allow access for older children, in which case you would still want to block the porn and morally unwelcome groups. The most offensive newsgroups are usually part of the 'alt' hierarchy of newsgroups – see Chapter 3 for more on the software that will help block newsgroups, and safety and privacy advice when using newsgroups.

Newsgroup basics

To access newsgroups you need special newsreader software and a standard Internet connection. If your ISP provided preconfigured software on a CD, there should be a newsreader program included. All the new web-browser suites of software include newsreaders, so it's easy to get started.

What are newsgroups? A newsgroup is a public discussion forum to which anyone can post a message. Any other visitor can read current and older messages. If you reply to an existing message, you are creating a 'thread' that groups together all the replies (and replies to replies) about one original message.

Some newsgroups, although public, tend to be run almost as a private meeting place for gangs of people. If you barge in and start chatting, you'll be flamed with rude emails – so always watch a newsgroup for a day to get the feel of it.

Where are newsgroups stored? When you add a message to a newsgroup, it's stored on a computer at your ISP called the news server or news feed. Because of the vast amount of information that's added to Usenet every day, most news servers can store only a few days' worth of messages. After this period, the oldest messages are deleted to make way for the new – a process called expiring. If you want to search Usenet for information, you should use a special search engine, such as Deja (http://www.deja.com), which has the vast storage capacity needed to record all the messages posted in all the groups.

There's no single computer that stores all the newsgroups. Instead the news servers at every ISP swap information to ensure that they are all up to date. If you post a message, it'll appear instantly in the

ewsgroup stored on your ISP's news server, but it will take a few
econds (or minutes) before it is copied to all the other news
ervers in the area. Over the next few hours, your message will be
utomatically copied to all the news servers across the world.

Which newsgroups can I access? No ISP will give you full run of the
0,000 different groups (it takes up too much hard-disk space on
heir servers), so they will probably drop newsgroups in a foreign
anguage (Chinese, German, Spanish) or remove newsgroups
bout porn or antisocial material. If you particularly want a group
hat's not been made available, try asking your ISP to provide a
articular group; most will oblige.

Getting started
You don't need much to get going on the Usenet: just a
onnection to the Internet and a newsreader program. The main
veb browser applications from Microsoft and Netscape both
nclude a newsreader. Microsoft's reader is part of its Outlook
xpress program (which also manages your email) – you can
download OE from the http://www.microsoft.com site. There are
many alternative newsgroup readers that provide different sets of
eatures and, if you've the time, try them out – they're usually all
ree – to see which you prefer.

> The first time you connect your newsreader to your ISP's
> news server, the software will download the names of all
> the newsgroups you can access. It can take up to ten
> minutes for this information to download, so be patient.

Setting up your newsgroup reader
you used a special setup CD-ROM from your ISP or configured your
veb browser using the setup Wizard or Assistant, it's almost
ertain that your newsgroup reader is ready to use; if not, see the
ox on how to configure your software.

If you use Microsoft's IE web browser, you'll find that the newsgroup reader is part of the main email program, Outlook Express. Start this by choosing the Tools/Mail&News/Read News menu option. In Netscape's browser, you'll need to start the Messenger email program (Communicator/Messenger) and then click on the news server listed in the left-hand pane.

How to configure your newsgroup reader

Before you can use your newsgroup reader software, it needs to be configured. This is very similar to setting up email software. You will need the name of the special computer that your ISP uses to store all the newsgroup messages (called the newsgroup server). This should be in your welcome pack from your ISP. You will also need your normal Internet login user name and password.

1 Start the newsgroup reader program (Outlook Express or Messenger). The first time you start the software, it should ask you to type in the name of the newsgroup server, your user name and password.

2 If the software does not ask you for this information, you'll need to find the setup screen. In Netscape, select the Edit/Preferences menu option and choose the Mail & Groups/Groups Server option from the list on the left-hand side. In Microsoft, choose the Tools/Accounts menu option and click on the News page tab. Click on the Add button on the right-hand side.

3 Type in the name of the newsgroup server – as supplied by your ISP. It should start with the word 'news' and will look something like 'news.virgin.net' (for Virgin Net ISP users).

4 Click on OK and the software will add this newsgroup server as an icon at the bottom of the list displayed on the left-hand side of the software.

Finding a newsgroup Once you have the current list of newsgroups in your news-reader software, you can browse through looking for something that sounds interesting, or use your reader's filter function to narrow down the list to group titles that contain a particular word. However, until you visit the group, you'll never know quite how active, friendly or useful it really is.

A good way to find a newsgroup that's of interest is to use a specialist search engine, such as Deja (http://www.deja.com) or Tile.Net (http://www.tile.net) to search through archives of newsgroup messages – you'll soon see which newsgroups are relevant. Alternatively, search for a newsgroup by its founder's description at http://alabanza.com/kabacoff/Inter-Links/.

Order from chaos – hierarchies

Newsgroups are divided into seven broad categories, called hierarchies. These are:

comp computer-related newsgroups

misc any groups that don't fit into the other categories

news discussions about the Usenet itself

rec hobbies and sports

sci science-orientated discussion

soc social issues

talk discussion of (generally controversial) issues

In addition to these seven main categories, there is an eighth, rogue, category called 'alt', which contains a wild range of newsgroups and is responsible for the contentious and lewd reputation of Usenet.

Each of the main hierarchies is divided into subcategories. For example, in the 'comp' hierarchy, there are the 'comp.ibm' and 'comp.mac' categories, which contain newsgroups about PCs and Macintosh computers. Each level of organisation is separated by a full stop; it makes it a little easier for you to have a good stab at guessing what a newsgroup is all about. For example, the rec.music.classical newsgroup is devoted to discussion of classical music as entertainment (rather than as a profession or business).

Identifying yourself Every message posted to a newsgroup has the sender's email address. It's up to the sender to decide whether to supply a real or a fake email address. Most newsgroup users really don't want to be identified, so they provide a false email address. In fact, this isn't the crime you might imagine, but a perfectly reasonable response to a major problem.

Unscrupulous mail-shot companies trawl through newsgroups picking up the email addresses and adding these to a mailing list that's then sold on. You can guarantee that if you post a message under your real email address, you'll soon be bombarded with junk mail and spam.

If you think you're anonymous when you're on the net, just visit **http://www.privacy.net/analyze/** and see how much personal information you're already showing in public.

When you configure your newsgroup reader, you need to enter an email address to identify your postings. If you have an Internet account with the option of several email addresses, you could use a spare address just for your newsgroup activity. Or, better still, sign up for a free email account with Bigfoot, Hotmail or Excite! and use this, or you might decide to enter a bogus address – you'll see other users using a variety of techniques to dodge the spam merchants.

Reading and posting
Newsgroup readers look and work in a very similar way to an email program: on the left there's usually a list of the newsgroups (or the

selection that you have chosen as interesting) and on the right you'll see the title line of the latest postings. Click on title and the full message is displayed.

If an entry starts a new topic of discussion, it's called a new thread. The first entry has a small square beside it on the left, to show it's the start of a thread. Click on the square and you'll see all the other messages listed beneath it that were sent in reply. (You can also configure your reader to display postings in strict date order, but then you'll lose the structure of the threads.)

You can post a new message or reply to an existing message in exactly the same way as creating an email. If you're using Microsoft Outlook Express or Netscape Communicator, you'll find the icons for email and newsgroup in the same place – if you've sent an email message, you'll feel right at home.

So you don't make a complete nitwit of yourself with your first posting – there are a couple of newsgroups dedicated to newcomers trying out the system: alt.test and misc.test are the main stamping grounds of newbies. You won't get flamed or subjected to silliness – and you should even receive a nice email in return for your test message.

You are strongly advised to 'lurk' for a while – read the messages without posting any new ones – to get the feel of a newsgroup before posting messages to it.

Subscribing to newsgroups

There are way too many newsgroups to try to read them all. Instead, you can use your newsreader to subscribe to the few that are of interest. This ensures that you'll keep up to date with new messages posted to these newsgroups – you can still view any other group whenever you want, but for day-to-day work, try to limit yourself to just a few favourite groups. Here's how to subscribe to a newsgroup:

1 In Outlook Express, click on the Newsgroups button to see a complete list of all the groups available on your server.

2 You can narrow this list down by typing in a key word in the field at the top of the window. If you're interested in toy cars, type in 'cars' and you'll see a cut-down list of the few dozen groups covering car-related topics.

3 Select the group that's of interest and click on the Subscribe button. The group is added to the list on the left of the screen, just below the name of your news server.

4 Now, if you want to view the messages in this group, click on the group name on the left-hand side of the screen. Outlook will always keep the list of messages in this group up to date, till you unsubscribe.

Reading offline Reading newsgroup messages when you're connected to the Internet is ideal, but it'll hike up your phone bill. The alternative is to download all the new messages from your selected newsgroups, then log off and read them offline. If you post any replies, wait till you've read all the messages, then dial up and send off your new messages.

All the main newsreader programs support reading messages offline – but some make it harder than others. For example, Microsoft's Outlook newsreader is good at managing on- and offline access to newsgroups. If you want offline access, subscribe to the newsgroup then select the Synchronize button to download the entire message base for this group.

Newsgroups: the ground rules
You can say pretty much what you like in a newsgroup, so long as it's related to the subject. But (and this is a big 'but') you must observe some basic etiquette when posting to any newsgroup. Some of the rules are simply good manners, while others are

specified by the newsgroup – but the majority are for your own protection.

1   Be very sure that your children are adult enough to understand the risks when using newsgroups.

2   If your children want to subscribe to a newsgroup, check it out yourself first. To prevent children subscribing to groups that contain porn or antisocial material, use a filter program (see page 25) to block access.

3   When you post a message, never give out your home phone number or any other personal details. If you want to chat to someone in particular, use email or instant messaging (see Chapter 6: 'Electronic Mail') – not a public forum that puts your personal life in front of millions of potential loons.

4   It's a wise precaution to use a dud or alternative email address for your newsgroup postings. Set up a free email account with Hotmail or Excite! – there's too much misuse of email addresses from newsgroups.

5   Don't post the same message to a whole mass of newsgroups – called spamming – because it'll annoy people in all the groups.

6   Make sure your postings are relevant to the group. If you're not sure, read the FAQ (frequently asked questions) for the group, which are sometimes posted as a message. The FAQ message will spell out the ground rules and acceptable subjects for discussion. If you can't find this FAQ message, visit http://www.faqs.org for a list of all the FAQs for all the newsgroups.

7   When you post a message, don't SHOUT in capitals – you'll get a barrage of rude messages back (called flaming).

8   Use smileys when you're trying to be funny or sarcastic.
    Not everyone shares your highly developed sense of
    humour and they may need prompting. Just make sure you
    don't use more than a couple of smileys per message.

9   Don't reply to a provocative or deliberately argumentative
    message (a flame), or you'll start a flame war (slanging match).

10 Parents should block the ability to download images or
    programs via Usenet – they're likely to be pornographic,
    pirated or infected with a virus.

//CHAT

Chat on the Internet provides some of the best fun around –
particularly for kids. Normally, when you're using the Internet,
there's a delayed reaction to anything you type in. Even when you
use a newsgroup, it can take an hour or even a day before
someone comments on your message. Chat changes this. With its
instant response, it sits somewhere between a gossipy telephone
call and the verbal barrage from contentious talk in a crowded
room full of strangers.

Find out about scheduled chats with movie stars, pop stars and
other celebrities – check **http://www.yack.com** or **http://www.liszt.com** for
details.

There are several different systems that let you chat to your friends
or join in a roomful of strangers. Either way, it's live: as you type
out a message on your keyboard, it's immediately displayed on
everyone else's screen. If you want to have a quiet chinwag with a
pal, use an instant messaging system – but you both need to run
the same special software and be online at the same time.
Alternatively, take your chances and join in IRC (Internet relay chat)
– a vast collection of chat rooms (called channels), each specialising
in letting you talk about a particular subject.

Instant messaging is fun for children: they can chat to pals or new Internet pen pals – if you set it up correctly and if they follow the ground rules. IRC is not really a place for young children and we would generally advise that you don't let kids under sixteen access to IRC.

Chat and children

Talking to strangers is never a good idea for any children, especially young ones. Since this is exactly what online chat is all about, you need to be very careful when allowing your children to access this feature. Generally, IRC and open, public chat sessions can be full of bad language (at best) and can include harassment, molesting, antisocial, racial or obscene messages.

By contrast, having a private chat with pals from school using instant messaging can be great fun. Look to Chapter 3 for details on how parents should monitor any type of chat, how to block access and advice on avoiding the dangers of chat.

//IRC (INTERNET RELAY CHAT)

IRC is where the net-heads chat till dawn. Much of it is very adult in language and on the whole, it's not a good area of the Internet for young children to roam. However, as parents, you may fancy a chat, or your older teenagers may be ready to join in – so here's what it's all about.

Like newsgroups, IRC is divided into separate discussion groups – called channels. Unlike newsgroups, anything you type in on your computer will instantly appear on every other channel member's screen. Remember, it's all live and in front of a small audience (if you want a one-to-one chat, try instant messaging).

Getting started

To use IRC you'll need a standard Internet connection and an IRC program. Unusually, IRC programs (normally called clients) aren't bundled in with the main web browsers – instead, you'll probably need to download a program from the web. The most popular PC program is mIRC (free from http://www.mirc.com), and for the Mac it's IRCle (from http://www.ircle.com) or ChatNet (from http://www .elsinc.com).

First off, you'll notice that IRC programs are poor relations in snappy user-interface design. They're stuck in the late 80s, when the technology evolved. There's nothing wrong with this, but, if you've used only Windows 98, you'll find it clunky.

Setting up IRC If you received a CD-ROM starter pack from your ISP, there's sure to be an IRC client on there. If not, download a version (see above for the addresses of mIRC and IRCle). When you first run the program, you'll be prompted to type in your nickname and email address – type in a name you want to use as a nickname (one that's displayed to other users in the channel), your real name and your normal email address. Some IRC servers check that your email address is correct and will refuse you entry if you enter a fake. You also need to enter the name of a computer that allows chatting – the software will have a list of friendly computers – called 'IRC chat servers'. Choose one from the File menu list. (Alternatively, your ISP may host an IRC chat server that will have local users, or you can visit Liszt [www.liszt.com], which has a database of independent IRC chat servers).

When you choose the chat server, you'll see a list of the various channels (discussion groups) available at the moment. Once you've selected a channel, you'll see the messages from other members displayed in one part of the screen – the other sections of the screen show the list of channels and the nicknames of the users in this channel. To start with, just spend a couple of minutes reading the conversations. It can be rather daunting to leap in without an introduction, but stick with it – it's great fun.

Your first chat It can be a little frightening entering your first IRC session, so let's take it step by step. When you link to the chat server, you'll see a list of channels available; channel names start with a '#' symbol. Each channel is just a forum that's been created by another user to chat about some particular topic (there may be a one-line description next to the channel name to give you a clue).

Find a channel that looks interesting or active (the number of other people chatting in the channel is displayed just after its name). To enter, double-click on the channel name. You're immediately in a live session; your nickname has been broadcast to the other members in the channel and you'll see their comments flying back and forth in different colours in one window of the IRC program. On the right of the comments should be a list of the other members who are in the channel. Read what's going on then just join in if you want to. After a few minutes, you'll get into the swing of it.

Moderation IRC channels are a splendid example of self-moderation. If you do or say something stupid or offensive, you'll be kicked off the channel (with the '/KICK' command) by one of the operators who set up the channel (their nicknames start with an '@').

Some IRC servers and channels use bots – software that monitors what's said and automatically kicks a user off the channel if they swear or use bad language. If you are kicked off, it's a warning – but there's nothing to stop you joining the group again immediately.

Language The language used in IRC channels is a kind of super-shorthand. If you're trying to type as fast as you can think and talk, you'll try to devise as many short cuts as possible. There's a lot of 'how r u' and so on. As with reading classified ads, it takes a while to get into the swing of things. We've seen some of the abbreviations used with email. Here are some of the more common abbreviations you may encounter while chatting – and they're useful for email as well.

AFAIK – as far as I know

BBL – be back later

BFN – bye for now

BRB – be right back

BTW – by the way

FWIW – for what it's worth

FYI – for your information

GR8 – great

IIRC – if I recall correctly

IMHO – (sarcastically) in my humble opinion

IMO – in my opinion

LOL – laughing out loud

M8 – mate

NP – no problem

ROFL/ROTFL – rolls on (the) floor laughing

RTFM – read the effing manual

TTFN – ta-ta for now

WB – welcome back

There are also a lot of smileys scattered around to give a better idea of emotions meant by a joke or comment. See page 74 in Chapter 6 on email for some of the most commonly used smileys.

Essential advice As with a newsgroup, there's not much that you cannot say in a chat channel – so long as it's appropriate to the channel you're in. Even swearing is generally OK and used as part of the chat rather than an insult. But do, please, follow these basic rules, and make sure your children know them too.

1   Don't give out any personal information – such as your age, address, phone number, or school.

2   Don't agree to meet anyone in real time whom you've talked to via IRC, unless it's a known friend.

3   If someone's rude to you, quit the session. Don't reply or take the bait.

4   If someone suggests typing in any command, don't unless you know what it does. Many users have hours of fun leading newbies astray.

5   Don't hassle anyone else in the channel for anything – you wouldn't like it.

6   Relax and be yourself. The other users can generally tell if you're a nervous new user.

7   If you download a program via IRC, then virus-check it before you run it.

To find out more about the rules of IRC, how to protect yourself and the etiquette, visit the excellent IRChelp site (**http://www.irchelp.org**).

//INSTANT MESSAGING

IRC has its place as an open forum, but if you want a private chat with your pals there's nothing to beat instant messaging. The idea's simple: special software will tell you the moment a friend has connected to the Internet and is available for a natter.

At the start of the revolution was the giant Internet provider, AOL. Since its charging scheme required it to keep track of when users logged on and off, it was easy to extend this to a system that could let you know when a fellow user was online. However, no other Internet provider keeps track of who's logged on to their server.

A new and very popular system has solved this problem. ICQ ('I seek you', geddit?). It's so successful that there are plenty of rivals (including programs from Yahoo!, iChat and PowWow, and a modified version of the AOL software that's also supplied with the Netscape browser) that all work in the same way. You have to download the utility software required, install it and register your nickname and email address at a central site. From now on, whenever you connect to the net, you'll get an immediate check on who else is online and ready to chat.

Unlike the case with IRC, you can set up ICQ so that it provides a degree of privacy. You don't have to broadcast to the world that you're waiting to chat: instead you can limit this news to a list of friends or colleagues. When they connect, have a one-on-one or all gossip away in your private meeting room.

Warnings for children

Instant messaging is a great, fun way to chat with friends – but it's just as easy to set up a private conversation with a total stranger. It's not just like dialling a wrong number on the phone: these people want to talk to anyone – the problem is that you've no idea who they are.

When you sign up for any of the instant-messaging systems, you are given a unique number or address. You are also asked if you want to broadcast to strangers the fact that you're online and available for a chat. Two key points for children: (1) don't give out your unique number to strangers; (2) set up your chat software so that your presence is not broadcast automatically to other users. Parents should be quite sure that they understand how the software works and how to set it up correctly to block strangers (see Chapter 3 for more details).

When you do use chat, as with any other public Internet system, there are a few basic guidelines to follow to be sure you're not at risk:

- children shouldn't give out any personal information about their name, address, school, phone number or real email address.

- children shouldn't agree to meet anyone in the real world, unless accompanied by parents or other responsible adult.

- chat software should be set up to ensure your name and address are not broadcast to strangers.

- if children get a nasty or obscene message, they should tell their parents or guardians immediately – they can call the ISP and get the user traced and blocked.

Get talking with instant messaging

Instant messaging (IM) has rapidly become one of the most popular ways of chatting to other users. You can decide if you want to have a private chat with a friend or enter a free-for-all session with a group of strangers. Best of all, you can set up IM so that it alerts you when a friend or colleague is online and ready to chat.

Make sure that you understand the dangers involved with instant messaging – it's not something that you should install for all members of the family. Read Chapter 3 for details of how to protect your family in this potentially dangerous part of the internet.

Getting started Choosing a system to use is not too difficult since, out of the list of instant messaging systems available, the original ICQ still beats the rest on its ease of use and established user base – though AOL Instant Messaging and Yahoo! Pager both come close.

Setting it up To start chatting with instant messaging, you'll need some special software and a connection to the Internet. Unlike IRC and newsgroups, each type of IM software uses a different system of sending messages, so generally they are incompatible. Although there are dozens of different programs available, three dominate. ICQ, AOL and Yahoo! Pager have the largest number of users and are easy to use. If you use AOL or the latest version of the Netscape browser, you are already set up to use AOL Instant Messaging. If you are with another ISP, you'll have to download one of the special software systems, but it's free.

One of the benefits of instant messaging is that the better systems include a directory of users, making it relatively easy to locate a friend or colleague for a chat. However, this means that you'll have to enter more information to configure the software – and your entry in the directory. To get started, download the software from AOL (http://www.aol.co.uk/aim), ICQ (http://www.icq.com) or Yahoo! (http://www.yahoo.com). When you install the software on your computer, the program will ask you to type in your real name, nickname, email address and (optionally) a description of yourself or your interests.

Next, you need to set up the level of privacy you want to use – do you want to allow any other user to call you for a chat or do you want to restrict this list to just a few known friends?

The chat software will sit quietly in the background while you surf with your web browser or check your email – until another user asks you if you want to chat. It'll pop up and tell you who's calling and give you the option to start a conversation.

Using chat

Unlike IRC, there's really very little to learn about instant messaging. Once you've entered your personal details (remember, these are stored in a public directory to help other users find you), the software just sits in the background, waiting for a call. If you've decided to allow incoming calls, other users can page you and ask if you want to chat. You can ignore the request or start a conversation.

If you want to talk, it's as easy to find someone to chat to. Either ask the software to pick someone at random or check if a friend is online. If either wants to chat, you'll see a little window appear – type and the message is sent direct to their computer.

INTERNET TELEPHONES

Typing out chat is all very well, but you can't beat a real conversation. You can make phone calls over the Internet, talking and listening to another user. And, with just a little extra hardware, you can even support a videophone link so you can see the person at the other end.

Not only is it possible to hold a normal conversation with another user over the Internet, you can even link to the regular phone system and place calls to anyone with a phone. Paradoxically, it's cheaper to use your computer to convert your voice into numbers, then convert these back into sound to send over a standard phone line, than to place a long-distance call over the phone. The quality is sometimes patchy and you may suffer an echo on the line but, with the right software, you will experience a remarkably clear line.

Now pity the poor telcos as they watch their profits disappear. But not too much: some countries have now banned Internet telephone calls (notably the Czech Republic, Hungary, Iceland and Portugal) because it's draining their revenue.

How Internet telephony works

To make a call over the Internet, you'll need a sound card, microphone and speakers installed in your computer. When you speak into the microphone, the sound card converts this into digital form and the telephony software compresses your speech into a very compact form, then sends it over the Internet to the recipient. It's rather like a chat session, except you're sending sound data instead of text.

One of the main jobs of the software is to try to regulate the flow of data to a steady stream. The recipient needs the same software and a sound card, microphone and speaker to decompress and play back your voice. Sometimes the Internet flies, at other times it crawls, and, if you're trying to send speech along this route, you're never sure if you'll get brilliant quality or break-up and echo. Some telephony systems can direct your call to a real telephone number rather than another computer user – but you'll need to pay a subscription.

You can make calls from your computer to a real phone. You'll need to use a gateway that links the Internet to the phone system. These are rarely free and you may need to subscribe or put down a deposit before you can run up a phone bill.

The costs

If you stick to calls to other users on the Internet, you'll pay only your usual phone costs to your telco. However, if you plan to dial out to a friend with a regular phone, you'll need to subscribe to a service that links the Internet to the phone system. These companies tend to change their rules – and names – even more often than other web services, so the simplest way to find them is to type in 'internet phone' in your search engine.

What you need

To make a phone call over the net is remarkably easy. If your computer has a sound card, microphone and speakers, and a fast modem (better than 28.8Kbps), then you're all set.

In addition to a standard Internet connection, you need special software that connects you to another user or acts as an exchange to a real phone. The latest web browsers have basic functions built in, but it's far easier to use a specialist program. Some you can download for free, others are sold commercially.

//ADDRESS BOOK

Newsgroup Readers

There's not much point switching from your web browser's integrated newsreader, unless you want a change of view. If you do, here are stand-alone programs that'll do the job.

Agent (PC)	http://www.forteinc.com
Gravity (PC)	http://www.microplanet.com
Hogwasher (Mac)	http://www.asar.com
Messenger (PC and Mac)	http://www.netscape.com
News Rover (PC)	http://www.newsrover.com
NewsWatcher (Mac)	http://www.filez.com
News Xpress (PC)	http://www.download.com
Outlook Express (PC and Mac)	http://www.microsoft.com

Finding and Searching Newsgroups

The major search engines now extend their reach to the Usenet but you can also use one of the specialist search engines below.

Deja	http://www.deja.com
Newsgroup Directory	http://Tile.net/news
Remarq	http://www.remarq.com

FAQ   **http://www.faqs.org**

Lists the FAQs for all the newsgroups in Usenet – check out what you can and can't say before you join in.

Usenet Info Center   **http://metalab.unc.edu/usenet-i/**

Links to newsgroup FAQs, search tools and support.

IRC Software

IRCle (Mac)   **http://www.ircle.com**
ChatNet (PC)   **http://www.elsinc.com**
mIRC (PC)   **http://www.mirc.com**
Liszt   **http://www.liszt.com**

Lets you search for an IRC server – or just use the default servers in your IRC client (you may also find there are channels supplied by your Internet provider).

Instant-Messaging Software

AOL Instant Messenger   **http://www.netscape.com**
iChat   **http://www.ichat.com**
ICQ   **http://www.icq.com**
PowWow   **http://www.tribal.com**
Yahoo! Pager   **http://Pager.yahoo.com**

Internet Telephone Software

CuSeeMe   **http://www.cuseeme.com**
Internet Telephone   **http://www.vocaltec.com**
Net2Phone   **http://www.net2phone.com**
Netmeeting   **http://www.microsoft.com**

8//YOUR OWN WEBSITE

Why would you want to create your own website? Everyone has something to say to the world, and here a just a few examples of the reasons why other users have set up their own site.

* it's dead easy
* so that your distant relatives can get the latest news about you and see your latest photos
* to tell the world about how brilliant you are
* you've got a wonderful pony/dog/cat/rabbit/zoo and think the world should know
* you had a great holiday and want to share the photos and travel tips
* to proclaim your adoration of a film star, pop star, philosopher or model – and get to know who else shares your passion
* to show off your collection and get more contributions

See what other kids and families have published in their home pages: Yahooligans! and Kids' Space Connection both have directories of sites by children (see the Address Book at the end of this chapter for details).

Getting web space

The collection of pages that make up your website needs to be stored on an Internet server. If you keep your web pages on your computer, you're the only one who can enjoy their depth and vision. Publish them – 'upload' them – to an Internet server and the rest of the webbed world will be able to enjoy your wisdom.

Your ISP will provide you with a certain amount of free web space that you can use to store your website. Both free and charging ISPs will supply you with web space as part of your account. If you are using a free ISP (such as Freeserve or Virgin Net), then you pay nothing, but you cannot have your own domain name, nor can you drive a complex database or store vast archives of video footage. If you want your own domain name, you'll normally need to pay for the privilege – once to the domain registration company (see later, 'Getting a Domain') and a second time to the ISP. And if your site gets very successful you'll probably be thrown off for generating too much traffic. It's at this point that you can turn to a paid provider who will accommodate your vast and growing audience, and you'll be able to raise money to pay for it all through advertising or sponsorship.

What's acceptable?

Anything goes on the Internet, but that's not necessarily true of the company that's providing the disk space to store your website. All web-space providers have their own AUP (acceptable user policy), which spells out exactly what you can and cannot do with your account. Many won't let you sell products or run commercial sites from a free account. Others don't want offensive material. If you break the AUP, your account will be closed down and you'll have to find another provider.

How do I build it?

When you create a site, you are really creating a collection of individual, linked pages. Don't make the pages too long and try to keep all the information about one thing in one page. Think of the things you like and dislike about other pages that you've visited. Too much text, too many images, everything crammed into one page? Make sure that you don't fall into these traps, by splitting your information into separate, linked pages.

Designing the page is rather like using a sophisticated word processor: you can type in text, add headlines, change the fonts, add in images, animation – even video clips. All these different elements of a web page are described using a special set of codes called HTML (hypertext markup language) – so you need to use a program that can let you create pages using HTML commands.

The most flexible and powerful way to create a web page is to use a special web-page design program – but they are often expensive and can take a while to learn. However, you can get started using an up-to-date word-processor application – such as Word or WordPerfect. Use all the standard word-processor formatting features to produce a good-looking document, then use the software's File/Save As or Export feature to save any document as a web page. The program converts your commands to HTML and you now have a document that can be read by a web browser and put on the Internet.

Alternatively, use your web browser. Both Microsoft's IE and Netscape's Navigator include extra programs that let you create a simple web page. With IE, choose the Web Publishing Wizard; with Navigator, it's called Composer. Whichever you use, the software looks like a word processor and lets you type in and format text and graphics.

Don't go overboard with fonts, colours and images. Look at lots of other people's sites to see what works for you. Take a look at Yahoo! for the clean-design look, or Superbad (http://www.superbad.com) for a confusing deluge of cutting-edge techniques.

These two methods will get you started, but they are limited on features and your pages will look rather basic. Once you've got the bug, try some of the specialised web-page editing programs (often called web-authoring software), which give you complete control over all the parts of a web page. Most authoring software is sold as a commercial product, but you can download trial versions that will run for thirty days before you have to pay. Visit Builder (http://www.builder.com), WebMonkey (http://www.webmonkey.com) or Filez (http://www.filez.com) to download a time-limited demo of some of the main programs.

Getting to grips with HTML

HTML is the universal language that defines how your web page will appear whenever it's viewed over the Internet. It's a clumsy but simple system. Here are the basic HTML commands to get your started.

HTML commands consist of words or letters stored within a pair of angle brackets (< >). They are decoded by the web browser that formats the text that follows according to the HTML command. The HTML language is mostly made up of pairs of commands: one switches something on, the other switches it off. For example <B> switches on bold type, </B> switches it off. HTML commands can be written in either upper- or lowercase – it doesn't make any difference.

When you create a web page by typing in HTML commands, there are several key points to bear in mind:

- Every web page has to have the first and last lines to tell the web browser that it's dealing with a file containing HTML.

- There's a line that tells the browser the page title to display at the top of the browser window (the second line in the example below).

- Now you get on to the main body of the web page; we've just displayed a single line with some bold text.

- If you want to expand your page, add in extra text and commands between the <BODY> ... </BODY> commands – leave the rest alone.

To get you up and walking (you can never run with HTML), here's how to create a very simple page:

1   Start your word processor or text editor (Notepad in Windows, SimpleText on Mac). Type in the following lines:

2   <HTML>

3   <HEAD><TITLE>My first web page</TITLE></HEAD>

4   <BODY>Here's where you include the <B>text</B> and <B>images</B> for your page</BODY>

5   </HTML>

Save this new document as a text file called 'index.htm'. Now, start your web browser and select the File/Open menu option. Select this file you've just created to display the page. Alternatively, drag the file icon on to your web-browser icon and your browser will start and display the page automatically.

Experiment with HTML by using the different text formatting and hyperlink commands. Text can be displayed in different sizes, fonts, and typefaces:

> <B>this will be displayed in bold</B>
>
> <I>this will be in italics</I>
>
> <CENTER>this will be centred on the line</CENTER>
>
> <H1>Use the H codes to describe the size of the text – H1 is big, H7 is small</H1>

Any text will be displayed in the browser's default font – usually a Times Roman, serif font. To get full control over the font, use the <FONT> command: <FONT FACE="arial" SIZE="-1"> displays small text in an Arial font. (If the computer that's viewing this web page doesn't have the Arial font installed, it uses the nearest equivalent – in this case, a sans-serif font.)

The HTML convention ignores any blank lines or carriage returns that may be in your text. It just runs together into one block of text.

You have to insert codes to create line breaks: either use a paragraph <P> command to break a line of text and add a blank line or use the <BR> command to end a line.

Including images

To include an image on your page, use the <IMG> code. You need to store the image files either as GIF or JPEG format files (almost any paint program can save graphics to these two formats). Avoid other formats such as TIF, PCX or BMP file – they simply won't work.

Kids get all the best deals – visit AcmeCity (**http://www.acmecity.com/looneytunes/**) and get free web space and masses of Looney Tunes cartoon characters to jazz up your home page!

If you're using a word processor to create your page, use the Insert/Picture menu option to include an image. If you're using a web-page authoring program (or one of the extras that came with your web browser), such as FrontPage Express, to create your web page, just click on the Image icon in the toolbar and type in the name of the image file.

There's a balancing act when creating images for the web between image quality, image size and the time it'll take to display the picture. You want to try to create high-quality, colourful images that are stored in a file that's as small as possible – so are quick to download and display. Include too many images, or use files that are too big, and users will give up on your site. Most visitors don't like waiting more than twenty seconds for a page to display, so try to limit yourself to just two or three images for each page.

The size of an image file is determined by the number of colours used, the size of the image and the resolution. Image-editing programs – such as the popular shareware Paintshop Pro (**http://www.jasc.com**) – let you adjust all three till you reach the perfect balance between quality and file size.

Advice on images

1   Use the JPEG file format for photos.

2   Use GIF files for simple images that have fewer colours.

3   Reduce the resolution to a maximum of 72dpi.

4   You can usually cut down the palette of colours used to 16 or 256 colours.

5   Reduce the file size of any image to a maximum of 30–40Kb (this will probably take around 8–10 seconds to download with a reasonable 56Kbps modem).

6   If you want to use lots of images, keep them very simple to keep the total file size to 30–40Kb.

Adding Links The web was designed to make it let you link one page to another, or one site to another so that a user can follow the links and travel around the web. A link can be either a few words of text or even a picture; your mouse pointer changes to a pointing hand when it passes over a link.

If you're using a word processor to create your page, highlight the text you want to set as a hyperlink and choose the Insert/Hyperlink menu function – then type in the full address of the destination page. If you're using FrontPage Express or Netscape's web-browser-based design program, highlight the text and click on the link icon (it's a picture of a couple of segments of a chain link). Now type in the full address of the destination page.

Alternatively, you can add links anywhere in your web page by using the <A HREF> HTML code. This code is followed by the address to jump to and then the text or image that's to be the hotspot. The line

    <A HREF="http://www.yahoo.com">Visit Yahoo!</A>

Chapter 8//107

will display the words 'Visit Yahoo!' in the usual link style: underlined and in blue. Click on these words and you'll be transported directly to the Yahoo! site.

If you have divided up the information you want to publish into separate web pages, you'll need to add links between them so that visitors can navigate through the site and jump from one page to the next. To jump to a page within your site, use the commands with the name of the file that contains the page. For example, to jump to a page that's stored in a file called flowers.htm, you would use the HTML command:

```
<A HREF="flowers.htm">Click here to see the
flowers</A>
```

Turn an image into a hotspot by including the name of the image file instead of the text. To turn our 'flower.gif' image into a hotspot that will whisk you to the 'flowers.htm' page use the code:

```
<A HREF="flowers.htm"><IMG SRC="flower.gif"></A>
```

When you build your site, think what you would like if you visited such a site. Include plenty of resources – links to other similar sites – you're part of a community!

Layout Effective websites use a clear design and are easy to find your way around (navigate). Many people opt for a design with the contents list running down the left-hand side; some prefer to keep navigation information at the top of each page.

Early versions of HTML had few features to help you position text in a particular place on the page. Unlike a design or DTP program, HTML pioneers had to be happy with text displayed in one block. With new enhancements to the HTML language, you can now position blocks of text or images in a specific position on the screen. Some web browsers support these new layout features, others do not.

Tables are the simplest way of positioning text and pictures in a particular area of the page, and they work with all types of browser. The table has individual cells (like a spreadsheet) that can contain an image or text. For better control, use frames – these are now supported by just about all brands of browser. The newest system, called DHTML, makes use of CSS (cascading style sheets). Use CSS if you want to be at the cutting edge, but only visitors with the newest browsers will see anything.

Java and JavaScript

When creating a web page, you are not limited to HTML commands. There are several different ways of extending the features of HTML. Two of the better-known systems are called Java and JavaScript; both let you add extra features and effects to your web page.

Java is a sophisticated programming language that's used to create small programs (called applets) that can be run by a browser.

JavaScript is a kind of extension to HTML that lets you add natty effects to your web page. When a browser loads a web page, it will follow the HTML and JavaScript commands.

Start with JavaScript and visit sites devoted to the subject (http://www.javascript.com or http://www.webmonkey.com or http://www.builder.com) and try out the snippets of code that they offer. Half your visitors with compatible browsers will think your site sophisticated, the other half won't see the effects at all.

Different browsers

The war between Microsoft and Netscape to gain the upper ground in web browsers has been the primary force in the high-speed development of HTML and web-publishing technologies. Each company tries to outdo the other by introducing a new way of helping web designers create super sites, but then the other browser is left behind. This leapfrog game is still being played out and leads to plenty of problems for web designers.

If you use some JavaScript commands, only Microsoft's IE browser will recognise them. Netscape's Navigator won't display anything. Similarly, DHTML and CSS are supported in different ways by each browser.

If you want to cater for the widest audience, don't use the newest tricks. If you do, you'll alienate half your visitors. Visit the wonderful www.browserwatch.com site to find out the current state of the battle between the browsers.

Advanced features

As you visit websites on your travels, you may want to have the same feature on your site. How do you add a discussion group, search a database or ask users to fill out a form? The answer is create a special program to carry out these features and link it to your web page using a system called CGI (common gateway interface). It's complex, but the nub is that it lets your web page send information to a program you've written that runs on the server.

Most of these programs are written in an archaic language called Perl. You'll need to learn how to write commands in Perl and you'll need an ISP that lets you run Perl scripts in your web space (some ISPs call these 'CGI scripts'). Many of the free ISPs do not let you run Perl scripts. If your ISP doesn't let you run scripts, you can use a second ISP to run the scripts for you, but this is often slow and a lot of bother – it's generally easier just to change ISP to one that does support scripts.

The Perl language lets you build complex sites, such as shopping sites, even search engines; you can find out more by visiting http://www.perl.com – to try out some of the free Perl scripts that are available to anyone, visit http://www.freescripts.com or http://www.freecode.com.

If this sounds too complicated for words, try Microsoft's FrontPage web-design program. It includes 'bots' that let you add these advanced features to your site without any programming. The snag is that you'll need a web-space provider that supports FrontPage, and you'll probably have to pay for this.

How do I publish?

Once you have designed and created your website, you need to copy the individual files that make up each page and the images you have used to your part of the hard disk on your web-space provider's server computer. This is called publishing the site – but it's no more complicated than copying files from your hard disk to a floppy disk.

To copy any file from one computer to another, over the Internet, you need to use a system called FTP (file-transfer protocol). This is just a simple series of commands that let your computer tell the server computer that it wants to transfer a file. You'll need a special program that's rather like the Windows Explorer – there are dozens freely available from sites such as **http://www.shareware.com** (just search for 'ftp'). You need to configure the FTP program with the user name, password and the address of the area of web space on the server (probably called your URL or 'site path' or 'FTP path'); all three will be provided by the company that's hosting your site when you signed up. So let's hope you made a note of them!

If you are using any of the main web-page design programs (FrontPage, HotDog, PageMill, Dreamweaver and so on), you'll avoid direct contact with FTP: the page design software will do all the hard work for you.

Your own address

Sign up with any Internet provider and you will get access to the Internet and an allocation of web space where you can store your own website. Your website will have its own unique address (normally called its URL), which lets any other user find and view your site.

To get your own personal address, without the provider's name in there, means registering your own domain name. The simplest way to register your own domain name is to ask your Internet provider to do the work for you. A few now offer domain names for free (such as http://www.freenetname.co.uk), otherwise you'll pay an initial registration fee, then a yearly subscription of between £40 and £100 per year. But you cannot yet have your own domain name with any of the free web-space providers, nor with AOL or CompuServe.

Publicity for your site

You've built your site, it looks great – now you have to tell everyone about it. The first announcement is the easiest: make sure that you include your website address in your email signature.

Getting your site noticed takes a lot of effort – you'll probably spend more time promoting your site than you did designing it. The most important place to start is to try to register your site with all the major search engines. Each search engine and directory has a special form you can fill in to submit your site. In theory, all the big search engines – such as AltaVista and Excite! – will automatically find your new site using their robots, which trawl the web looking for new pages. But it can take several weeks for the robot to notice you and add you to the index, so it's worth telling them about your site.

There are hundreds of different search engines and directories and you could spend weeks visiting each to submit your site's details. To save time, you can use one of the automatic submission tools like Submit-It or Exploit – but you'll have to pay.

You should also send an email to the webmaster of other similar sites and ask if they will add a link to your page. If the subject's popular enough, there may be a web ring (a collection of sites linked together to help visitors) that you could join.

Make sure that if you write anything for a mailing list or

ewsgroup, your signature includes your website. And create a
anner advertisement for your site – the little horizontal ads that
ppear at the top of most sites. There are several co-operative
chemes that let you swap banner ads with other similar sites – you
lace their ad on your site, they'll do the same for you. The biggest
cheme is called LinkExchange (http://www.linkexchange.com)
nd is free to join.

ADDRESS BOOK

ites by Children

ids' Space Connection	http://www.ks-connection.org/
ahooligans!	http://www.yahooligans.com/
ersonal Home Pages	Around_the_World/
	Personal_Home_Pages/

raphics for Your Web Page

cmeCity	http://www.acmecity.com/
lipart.com	http://www.net-matrix.com/graphx/
on Mania	http://www.kidsdomain.com/icon/index.html

ur Family Web Page

amily Shoebox	http://www.familyshoebox.com
lyFamily.com	http://www.myfamily.com

dvice for Site Builders

uilder	http://www.builder.com
avaScript	http://www.javascript.com
ages that suck	http://www.pagesthatsuck.com
ebMonkey	http://www.webmonkey.com

Web-page Editors	
Dreamweaver	http://www.adobe.com
FrontPage	http://www.microsoft.com
HotDog	http://www.sausage.com
NetObjects	http://www.fusion.com
PageMill	http://www.adobe.com

Publicity	
Exploit	http://www.exploit.com
Submit It	http://www.submit-it.com

There are millions of websites on the Internet, many of them very unsuitable for children and family viewing. We've trawled through the web to find the best 1,000 sites – sites that work, are child-friendly and useful, and provide a great starting point to the subject.

In each section, we've also included a selection of Starting Points – directory sites that list other sites (for example, www.leisure-uk.co.uk is simply a directory of sites about theme parks, zoos and great places for family outings). If you want to explore, use these as a springboard.

Use these sites as a starting point for your travels; if there's something really great, please let us know (send an email to response@virgin-pub.co.uk). You might find that some of the company names have changed (Internet businesses seem to be bought and sold on a daily basis), but you should be automatically redirected to the new site.

ACTIVITIES AND COLOURING

You're tired, it's a wet weekend afternoon, and your toddler is getting fidgety. The Internet can help out with a mass of activities and pictures to colour in that will keep any preschool kid occupied. Most children love drawing and painting, but there are also ideas for making simple necklaces, things from old loo rolls or fun games and puzzles. And if all else fails, try a song – there are a couple of sites dedicated to singalong kids' karaoke!

Starting Points

Geokids
Activity Pages

http://www.geocities.com/ EnchantedForest/1254/

Mass of things to do (and sites to see) compiled by five enthusiastic kids.

Coloring Books   http://artforkids.tqn.com/
and Pages   msubcolor.htm
Good directory of sites filled with pictures to print out and colour in.

Kid's Channel   http://www.kids-channel.co.uk
Keep the kids amused with games, puzzles, activities, stories and
colouring projects.

Summer Fun   http://db.ok.bc.ca/summer/
Ideas for exhausted parents to entertain the small bouncy people.
Includes recipes (for indoor and outdoor cooking methods) that
have been submitted by other exhausted parents.

Activities

Berenstain Bears   http://www.berenstainbears.com/
Activities   learnfun.html
Beautifully drawn bears busying around their world invite you in for
puzzles, stories, and colouring.

Big Brainy Babies   http://www.brainybabies.com
Taxing puzzles for talented toddlers.

Billy Bear's Playground   http://www.billybear4kids.com
One bear's selection of games, activities and stories. The material's
great, but rough-and-ready design and banner ads spoil the effect

Cathy's   http://www.geocities.com/
Picnic   Heartland/7134/index.html
Stacked high with interactive stories, puzzles, games, and music –
but let down by crummy design.

Disney   http://www.disney.co.uk
Mickey's official home in the UK – animations, ideas for games, and
interactive stories.

Kids Channel   http://www.kids-channel.co.uk
Keeping the kids amused with games, puzzles, activities, stories and
colouring projects – but its competitor, Kids' Space, provides more.

Kids' Space   http://www.kids-space.org

Great collection of games, puzzles, activities and an online version of the Gallery in VisionOn – any child can submit a picture, music, or story to the gallery.

KinderCrafts   http://www.enchantedlearning.com/crafts/

Make a necklace, mask or paper hat – lots of ideas to keep preschool children busy.

Kites and   http://www.geocities.com/
Kite Flying   Colosseum/4569/

All about kites – how they were developed and how to fly them.

Nikolai's Web Site   http://www.nikolai.com

Clubhouse-style family site with masses of activities, but the commercial ads spoil the atmosphere.

Paper Airplane Hangar   http://www.tycs.demon.co.uk/planes/

Just plane crazy. Masses of designs and ideas to get you off the ground.

ShooZoo   http://www.shoozoo.com

A bit of everything to keep kids busy. Get your own email address, set up a family message board, photo album, plus games and activities. You can also read stories, or write your own, play games and have fun with the help of cartoon animals.

Squigly's Playhouse   http://www.squiglysplayhouse.com

Lots of jokes, quizzes and brain-teasers to help while away the hours.

Time for Teletubbies!   http://www.bbc.co.uk/teletubbies/

Ehh-ohh, Tinky Winky. The four chubby friends provide games and ideas to help one- to three-year-olds to learn.

Winnie the Pooh and Pals   http://www.winniethepooh.co.uk

Wonderful site with games, puzzles, recipes, stories and poems about ... well, about Pooh. Also worth visiting is the similar, charming Pooh Corner (http://www.gironet.nl/home/awouters/).

World Village Kidz   http://www.worldvillage.com/kidz
A friendly welcome for pre-teen children who'll find games,
puzzles, homework helpers, comics and jokes.

Colouring

Bonus.com   http://www.bonus.com
A fantastic range of fun activities and stuff to colour in – but the
music will drive you up the wall.

Club Humongous   http://www.humongous.com
Color Me!   clubhe/color/coloractivity.htm
Sharpen your pencils – here are games, puzzles and pictures to
print out and colour in.

Coloring.com   http://www.coloring.com
Save paper, colour in online with the amazing technical trickery of
this site. Shame about the rather odd range of pictures.

Crayola   http://www.crayola.com
Select, print out, colour in. Perfect rainy-day fun, stories and
games.

Funorama   http://www.funorama.com
Lots to read, do and colour in from this multitalented children's
bookshop.

Zini's Activity Page   http://www.incwell.com/Zini
Find the crayons, it's colour-in time – dozens of nicely drawn pages,
puzzles and mazes to print and use.

Singing

Looney Tunes   http://www.kids.warnerbros.com
Karaoke   karaoke
Sing along with your fave cartoon characters – rather like the uncle
who gives your son a drum, this site will change your home's noise
levels.

KIDiddles http://www.kididdles.com

Little MoJo mouse is in charge of providing lyrics to all the popular children's songs.

//BABIES AND PREGNANCY

From pregnancy to first nappy, the Internet maps out the entire process – often in more detail than is strictly necessary. This section is dominated by vast catch-all baby sites packed with masses of advice about your health, the baby's health, how to look after it, what to do when it arrives and even what to call it. In short, there's advice on everything from cramps in pregnancy to the first burp.

Starting Points

Baby Directory http://www.babydirectory.com

An essential bookmark for any parent. Absolutely everything you need to know about pregnancy, babies, toddlers and children under five.

Babyhood http://www.babyhood.com

Get a free home page for your tiny tot; the rest of the site – dedicated to under-twos – has advice and support but is not up to Baby World standards.

Baby World http://www.babyworld.co.uk

First stop for anyone who wants children or has just received their first dribbling, howling bundle of joy.

Supplies

Babies Я Us http://www.babiesrus.co.uk

Everything to carry, clothe, feed and mop up after your new baby – from the Toys Я Us company.

Babycare Direct http://www.babycare-direct.co.uk

Good range of kit to help care for your new baby. A simple design hides a mass of products – similar range to Babies Я Us, but with better pictures and descriptions – unfortunately, currently no secure online ordering.

Baby Center   http://www.babycenter.com

Slick baby site that's packed with advice, features, shopping ideas and discussion groups for mums-to-be and new mums.

Babyworld   http://www.babyworld.co.uk

Almost the whole baby world is here – products, features, health news and special offers.

Bumble Bugs   http://www.bumblebugs.co.uk

Kit out babies and toddlers (up to age four) with clothes, toys and nursery essentials.

Character Warehouse   http://www.character-warehouse.com

Barney, Noddy, and the usual TV suspects are on offer.

Nappies Direct   http://www.nappies-direct.co.uk

Terry and flannel nappies direct from shop to bottom.

Over The Moon   http://www.zippi.co.uk/
Babywear   overthemoon/

Nice range of clothes and swimsuits for boys and girls from new to two.

Sunday Best   http://www.sundaybest.com/index.html

Long, flowing, white christening gowns and rompers for the elegant tot.

//BOOKS AND READING

Books are a great commodity for the web. You don't need to hold a vast amount of stock for browsing and you can slash prices and ship out with minimal effort. As a result, there are hundreds of bookshops online. The battle for supremacy among the biggest (Amazon, Barnes and Noble, AlphabetStreet and BOL) ensures that net prices are way below – often half – the price you'd pay in the High Street.

Smaller specialist bookshops, such as Books for Children and Funorama, compete with the giant booksellers by providing games for children and help for parents who are trying to choose a book. Alternatively, you can look to the review sites, such as Bookworm, which will tell you what's worth reading and what's best for young readers, and which generally categorise titles by age range.

Best of all, pay nothing and read one of the complete texts of a bedtime story, a novel or even a textbook that's been published directly to the net. They are also usually written by enthusiasts for enthusiasts and ensure you'll keep up to date with news, views, gossip, reviews and background detail on any subject. There are plenty of e-zines for children – many of the sites in the 'Kids Only' section have their own online magazine – dealing with (mostly) teen-orientated angst and problems.

Starting Points

Carol Hurst's Children's   http://www.carolhurst.com
Literature Site
Is it a good bedtime read or a scary story? Hundreds of children's books reviewed.

Bookworm books for kids   http://www.kidsreads.com
Recommended reads for your children (aged 6–12).

Children's Authors   http://www.acs.ucalgary.ca/
& Illustrators   ~dkbrown/authors.html
The creative folk behind your child's favourite books.

How a book   http://www.harperchildrens.com/
is made   howabook/
Wonderful illustrations and clear text show you ... er, how a book is made.

Just For Kids   http://www.geocities.com/
Who Love Books   ~abrown/kids.htm
Brilliant for bookish Bertie – an extensive collection of links to sites about children's authors and the book's characters.

The Literary http://www.people.virginia.edu/
Web ~jbh/litweb.html
Great writing is just a link away with this comprehensive listing of
hundreds of literary sites, neatly organised in a simple layout.

Booksellers

AlphabetStreet Books UK http://www.alphabetstreet.co.uk
One of the nicest, cheapest UK-based online booksellers.

Amazon http://www.amazon.co.uk
Everyone knows the Amazon bookstore – with good reason: it's
still the big cheese and its customer features are great. However
the rivals are catching up quickly. The US edition (**.com**) includes
everything from videos to gifts for sale, whereas the UK edition
(**.co.uk**) sticks to books, videos and CDs.

Barnes and Noble http://www.bn.com
The widest range of books on the net – the online bookshop
equivalent of the great US chain. There's even Starbucks coffee for
sale as you browse the widest range of titles available. It also sells
software, out-of-print titles and magazines.

Blackwells Bookshop http://bookshop.blackwell.co.uk
The high-street shop with an academic bent provides plenty of
high- and low-brow books for sale. There are very few discounts; it
prefers free postage and similar offers.

BOL http://www.uk.bol.com
The newest of the mega online bookshops, this edition covers the
European market and provides excellent listings for local titles plus
a few neat features such as your own bookshelf of favourite books.

Books for http://freespace.virgin.net/
Children books-for.children/
A real-life bookshop in London that's slowly coming online – a
small selection of key titles, but they'll find anything if you send
them an email.

Borders   http://www.borders.com
Vast bookshop chain provides masses of choice, with good service.

Children's Book Centre   http://www.childrensbookcentre.co.uk
Modest selection of titles and with few pictures, but neatly arranged by age group and with good descriptions.

Funorama   http://www.funorama.com
Lots to read, do and colour in with reviews of books by subject and age – from this multitalented children's bookshop.

The Book People   http://www.thebookpeople.co.uk
Online shop that's doing battle by discounting furiously. One of the nicest sites around – and very cheap: at the time of writing, these folk were offering discounts of 75%.

The Internet Book Shop   http://www.bookshop.co.uk
Part of WH Smith. There's the standard selection of over 1.4m titles plus CDs, videos and games. Their friendly cyber-clerk Jenny will keep you up to date with new titles as they are published.

Waterstones   http://www.waterstones.co.uk
Lots of choice in a smart-looking site. Neat feature is that you can exchange any book by nipping into your local Waterstones shop. Lots of savings and reader reviews.

Libraries

Internet Public Library   http://www.ipl.org
Stroll through the aisles, pick up your favourite book and download the full text for free. An often odd selection of books but that's the effect of copyright laws.

The British Library   http://portico.bl.uk
No, you cannot yet browse the entire collections stored in the BL, but at least you can search the catalogues and get background information from the site. For newer works, you can always try www.bn.com or the Internet Public Library.

The On-Line Books Page   http://www.cs.cmu.edu/books.htm
From Austen to Zola, you can download the complete texts of ove
9,000 books. Should keep you busy for a while.

E-zines

eZineCenter   http://www.ezinecenter.com
Find out how to run, manage, or just track down an e-zine.

InfoJump   http://www.infojump.com
Original thought on the web – if not always agreeable – is usuall
in e-zines. Search this huge database of almost every e-zine on th
web – but parents should make sure they vet the results carefully.

ZineZone   http://www.zinezone.com
Mass of e-zines about hundreds of different subjects created withi
one community site.

Stories

BeanTime Stories   http://www.meddybemps.com
Three stories from the magic island of Meddybemps – brigh
illustrations help the simple stories along, but music would help.

Harper   http://town.hall.org/Archives/radio.
Audio!   IMS/HarperAudio
Hardly for toddlers, but a great collection of audio stories from
classic authors (Brontë to Thurber) that are ideal for young adults
and their parents.

Internet Public   http://www.ipl.org/youth.
Library Story Hour   StoryHour.
Snuggle into a chair and listen to one of a dozen stories being read
– or sit up and read them yourself.

Stories to grow by   http://www.storiestogrowby.com
Folk and fairy tales from around the world, each with a mora
theme – but rather text heavy and no spoken stories.

tory Arts   http://www.storyarts.org

deas for teachers (and parents) to help make story time fun.

unnie BunnieZZ Storytellers   http://sunniebunniezz.com

tories, poems, puppets and puzzles from a gang of crazy bunny abbits.

heCase.com for Kids   http://www.thecase.com/kids/

cary, mysterious stories to read and detective puzzles to solve.

he Prince and I   http://www.nfb.ca/kids/

xciting adventures with our hero, the Prince, to teach elementary-evel words, writing and stories. Fantastic design and illustration rom Canada's National Film Board.

hekids.com   http://www.thekids.com

or children who love to spin a yarn: fables, adventure stories and airy tales with wonderful illustrations.

▼CLOTHES AND FASHION

Buying clothes on the net has taken off big time. Land's End, for xample, have a great virtual female model that can be adjusted to our shape and colouring, then dressed and fitted out online. But nake sure that you read the tips in the section on Shopping before nanding over your credit-card details.

Clothes Shopping

Boden   http://www.boden.co.uk

legant clothes for men, women and children from this slick mail-order supplier.

Clothing Connection   http://www.shoppersuniverse.com

A large online mall that includes men's and women's everyday or igh-fashion clothes plus children's clothes. A good place to start, but you'll find a better selection in specialist shops.

Designers Direct　　　　http://www.designersdirect.com

Kit yourself out in style for peanuts – all the top names at up to 75% off, delivered direct from the US in under a week.

Diesel UK Virtual Store　　　　http://www.diesel.co.uk

Not just denim from the trendy designers – shirts, jeans and scent for men and women. Cool design, and a few web-only offers.

Fashionmall.com　　　　http://www.fashionmall.com

A central mall to browse a wide range of clothes stores, from D&G to Liz Claiborne. A good place to start looking for clothes, but it's weak on beauty products.

Fat Face Online Store　　　　http://www.fatface.co.uk

Surf world hits web world with the funky range of outdoor and sports fleeces and shirts for the family. Online shoppers earn Fat Calories, which will add up to a 10% discount.

Freeman's　　　　http://www.freemans.com

Includes all the items from the famous catalogue – Ralph Lauren to Betty Jackson, Levi to Caterpillar. No special web offers, but you do get free delivery.

Kitbag　　　　http://www.kitbag.com

Keeping up with your football team's latest kit is now easier. But it's no cheaper.

Land's End　　　　http://www.landsend.com

Basic clothes, but with a terrific virtual model you can tailor to your size, shape and hair colouring before you dress her up.

L.L. Bean　　　　http://www.llbean.com

Famed outdoor clothing supplier – from chequered shirts to hunting boots – a super-slick site that keeps winning awards.

The GAP　　　　http://www.gap.com

You know the gear – basic cotton chinos, Ts and polo shirts – exactly like in the shopping centre, but without the crowds.

COMPUTERS

goes without saying that the Internet is a prime resource for
omputer buffs. You'll find product news, reviews and features
 help you get the best from your hardware and software. To find
our computer manufacturer's site, try entering their name
 trademark followed by '.com' or '.co.uk'. You'll hit Gateway,
ell, IBM, HP, Elonex, Dan, Time and others in this way. If you're
.uck, try a quick search in Yahoo!

 you spend your free time worrying about upgrades, bookmark
NET and ZDnet. Both provide features on new technologies and
ow to use them. For software addicts, hell-bent on trying out new
oftware, go straight to Filez or RocketDownload.

S suppliers

ou'll find the home to some of the keenest prices and sharpest
iscounts on new hardware and software. Unfortunately,
arranties and guarantees on both rarely extend outside the
ountry. If you're willing to risk this (you'd normally have to arrange
nd pay for repairs through a local repair company), you'll probably
ave to work hard to persuade them to ship outside the US.

oftware from the US

eyond.com	http://www.beyond.com
yberian Outpost	http://www.outpost.com
ookMark Software	http://www.bookmarksoftware.com
humbo.com	http://www.chumbo.com
gghead.com	http://www.egghead.com

ardware from the US

omputers4sure	http://www.computers4sure.com
yberian Outpost	http://www.outpost.com
Games	http://www.egames.com

Egghead.com	http://www.egghead.co◄
NECX	http://www.necx.co◄
NetBuyer	http://www.netbuyer.co◄

Starting Points

CNET   http://www.cnet.co◄

Packed with news, a vast shareware library, advice, and step-b
step instructions.

Webopedia home page   http://www.pcwebopedia.co◄

Should you be worried by the 'blue screen of death'? An onli◄
encyclopedia with this and thousands of other PC and web term
clearly defined.

ZDNet UK   http://www.zdnet.co.u◄

Should be any surfer's first stop for computing news, reviews ar
features from the expert computer-magazine publishers.

Computer Hardware

Dixon's   http://www.dixons.co.u◄

Anything that's for sale in the high street store is available online
that means TVs, hi-fi systems, PCs, fax machines and cameras.

Inmac   http://www.inmac.co.u◄

Well-stocked warehouse piled high with hardware and software
low prices and with great service.

Jungle   http://www.jungle.co◄

Smart shop packed with hardware, software, music and videos
low prices.

Microwarehouse   http://www.microwarehouse.co.u◄

Provides just about the best range of computer hardware, softwa
and accessories and a good price. Better range than Action, b◄
the search and catalogue is not quite as slick.

Morgan Computers   http://www.morgancomputers.co.uk
Cheap and cheerful end-of-line or used brand-name computers, printers and other office equipment.

TechWeb   http://www.techweb.com/shopper
Comprehensive database of computer hardware and software that'll help you decide what's best for you.

Custom Hardware

Order your custom-built computer from these manufacturers:

Apple Store	http://www.apple.com
Dell	http://www.dell.co.uk
Elonex	http://www.elonex.co.uk
Evesham Micros	http://www.evesham.com
Gateway 2000	http://www.gw2k.com
Tiny	http://www.tiny.co.uk
Viglen	http://www.viglen.co.uk

Software

CD Direct   http://www.cddirect.co.uk
Excellent range of software on CD – from games to office applications. Easy navigation, good budget titles and reviews.

Download.com   http://www.download.com
Buy and instantly download software to your computer – part of the impressive CNET resource site.

jungle.com   http://www.jungle.com
Sharp, snappy site full of software, hardware, videos, music and games at discount prices.

Macintouch   http://www.macintouch.com
Keep your Mac bug-free with the latest software fixes and updates.

Software Paradise   http://www.softwareparadise.co.uk
Over 100,000 software titles for sale at discount prices. Covers all

platforms from PC to Mac – and from developers around the world.
Very easy to use.

The Educational   **http://www.**
Software Company   **educational.co.uk**

Over 1,000 of the top educational software programs at reasonable
prices. There are decent descriptions for most entries and
recommendations help you pick the right program for your child's
age and level.

Updates   **http://www.updates.com**

Make sure all your applications are up to date – this free utility will
scan your hard disk to check what's installed, then tell you what
needs to be updated and how to do it.

Shareware

CNET   **http://www.cnet.com**

Everything you need to know about your PC and the software to
make it zing. There's news, lots of reviews, advice on fixing
problems, designing websites and a vast library of shareware.

Filez   **http://www.filez.com**

Claims to have the widest range of shareware files available to
download, but CNET wins on general coverage.

Rocketdownload.com   **http://www.rocketdownload.com**

Another good collection of shareware files to download – the big
difference here is that the files have all been rated and described
(saving you the annoyance of downloading junk).

Tucows Network   **http://www.tucows.com**

Great collection of all the software you'll ever need – neatly
arranged into categories. Rivals CNET in ease of use but without the
range of Filez.

DriverZone   http://www.driverzone.com

Drivers are tiny but vital bits of software that let your computer control your modem, hard disk, monitor or printer. Check here to make sure you've got the latest version or for advice on problems.

Help   http://www.free-help.com

Get help fast – ask an expert about your computer problem.

MacFixIt   http://www.macfixit.com

Help get your Mac working properly (for a change).

Modem Help   http://www.modemhelp.com

If you can get to this site, your modem's probably working. If it isn't, you'll wish you could.

My Desktop   http://www.mydesktop.com

Great advice supplied, together with news and features.

PC Mechanic   http://www.pcmech.com

Advice on how to upgrade or build your own PC.

SquareOneTech   http://www.squareonetech.com

A useful series of Internet guides that'll tell you almost as much as this book about getting online and using the net – the difference is you first have to work out how to get online to use the guides.

Tom's Hardware Guides   http://www.tomshardware.com

Tom the PC man provides news about hardware and software plus a series of reasonable guides about various bits of your PC.

Windows Annoyances   http://www.annoyances.org

What Microsoft didn't include in Windows and how to fix the irritating features they did include.

//COOKING AND FOOD

Take a break from fish fingers and baked beans, and get inspiration for tea time or dinner parties from the two biggest foodie sites on the web – Epicurious and Global Gourmet. You'll find features on ingredients, new ways to cook and thousands of recipes. Other sites, such as Classic Recipes, provide exactly what the name suggests, ensuring you'll never be left wondering how to knock up a gnocchi or serve up a sauce.

Once you know what you're cooking, order the food: you can do your full weekly shop at Tesco or Sainsbury's online, leaving the in store picker to deal with the Saturday crush, then deliver to you home. Alternatively, visit smaller specialist shops that provide a fantastic range of meat and veg.

Starting Points

BBC Food and Drink   http://www.bbc.co.uk/foodanddrink/
Top nosh without the irritating chatter of the presenters.

Classic Recipes   http://www.classicrecipes.com
The original core database of recipes is still there but it's now surrounded by so many other foodie sections, features and guide that it can be a little overwhelming.

Epicurious Food   http://food.epicurious.com
The message is 'If you eat, visit this site' – and it's not wrong. Vast site that shows just how much can be written about food, recipe and drink. It's US-centric – but, with this amount of information who cares?

Global Gourmet   http://www.globalgourmet.com
A good all-rounder for gourmets and gourmands – not quite up to Epicurious, but easy to manage.

Kitchenlink   http://www.kitchenlink.com
Great site stacked high with links to almost every worthwhile

culinary site on the web. Hardly a slick design, but a great place to start.

TuDocs http://www.tudocs.com

Thousands of cooking and food sites rated to help you explore without time-wasting. (And 'tu' stands for 'the ultimate', in case you wondered.)

Buying Food

Cheese http://www.cheese.com

Mild Cheddar, yes, but also over 500 smellier cheeses listed and arranged by name, taste and texture and country. A similarly extensive and obsessive (if not quite so polished) site is CheeseNet at http://www.wgx.com/cheesenet/

Organics Direct http://www.organicsdirect.com

Organic food, chocolates, and even socks are delivered anywhere in the UK.

Real Meat Company http://www.realmeat.co.uk

Caring farmers selling meat produced without chemicals – shop online for speedy delivery.

Sainsbury's http://www.sainsburys.co.uk

Online supermarket with a similar delivery charge to Tesco, but a different working method. First, visit your local store with a bar-code gun and build up your basic shopping list. Now you can order from the website – but it's painfully slow and often more reliable to phone.

Tesco http://www.tesco.co.uk

Rival to Sainsbury's delivery service. Similar delivery rates, but you choose your items from the virtual aisles – no need to visit a shop with a bar-code scanner. And you can even get a free Internet account.

Waitrose http://www.waitrosedirect.co.uk

Still limited to ordering wine, flowers and organic produce.

Guides and Magazines

Food and Drink   http://www.learn2.com/browse/foo_2tor.html
Boil an egg or clean a fish; the Learn2 site provides plenty of concise culinary how-tos for timid kitchen explorers.

Genetically modified world   http://gmworld.newscientist.com
Spot the difference between a GM tomato and a beach ball. Clear and impartial scientific coverage of all sides in the GM battle.

Jaffa Cakes   http://www.jaffacakes.co.uk
More than you ever wanted to know about the orange biscuits.

PastaRecipe.com   http://www.pastarecipe.com
Not difficult to guess this site's speciality. A good place to visit before tea time.

RecipeXchange   http://www.recipexchange.com
Database of recipes tried, tested and submitted by netters. Some are classic, some unusual, some revolting.

Restaurants.co.uk   http://www.restaurants.co.uk
Trying to find some place to eat? There are over 20,000 restaurants listed by area in Britain, and by style of food. But it delivers only name and contact details.

Veggies Unite!   http://www.vegweb.com
A safe haven for vegetarians. Over 3,000 recipes, features and discussion groups.

Winnie the Pooh   http://www.winniethepooh.co.uk/
and Pals   owlsrecipies.htm
Owl's splendid recipes for Pooh pancakes, jam tarts and brownies.

World of   http://members.tripod.com/
Recipes   ~WorldRecipes/recipe_links.htm
An enthusiastic cook (with obviously a very hungry family) has compiled a comprehensive range of recipes. If you want to stick to tried and tested dishes, use RecipeXchange.

//EDUCATION

Choose the best school, find a university place, check the latest directives from the government – the web is invaluable for parents who want to keep in touch with their children's education.

To find out what your children should be studying and how the government expects both students and schools to perform, use the official Qualifications and National Curriculum site or the similar National Grid for Learning and its parent DfEE site. If you're trying to find out about local schools, use the UpMyStreet (www.upmystreet.co.uk) reference site to show you what's available. For parents after an independent education for their child, Schools Net lists almost all in the country. And if you are considering higher education, use the UCAS site to help find a place in a university or college.

Starting Points

Argosphere   http://www.argosphere.net
Find your school's site in the directory, learn with the educational activities, or pay for a full online tutorial to help you swot up.

BBC Education   http://www.bbc.co.uk/education/
Vast collection of advice for parents, students and teachers, news about the National Curriculum, for children and even help with homework.

Directory for UK   http://www.mailbase.
Higher Education   ac.uk/juga/
As it suggests, a directory of university and college websites.

EduWeb   http://www.eduweb.co.uk
Provides a central location for websites created by the teachers and pupils from hundreds of schools around the UK.

Freeserve Education   http://www.freeserve.net/education/
Everything that's relevant to education. A great resource that's available to anyone – you don't have to join Freeserve first.

TES Learnfree   http://www.learnfree.co.uk
News, reports and guides for teachers, parents and students
(in that order).

___

Official

National Grid for Learning   http://www.ngfl.gov.uk
The government's very good attempt to provide online learning
resources that help parents with their children's education; you'll
need to register, but it's free. If you want school assessments or
how to complain to your LEA, try the DfEE site at http://www.
dfee.gov.uk/par_cent/.

National Curriculum   http://www.dfee.gov.uk/nc/
Official line on the key stages for your child's education.

Qualifications and Curriculum Authority http://www.qca.org.uk
Find out what your child should be studying and the key stage
examinations the poor thing will have to face – from the official UK
organisation responsible for managing the different stages in your
child's development.

Scottish Qualifications Authority   http://www.sqa.org.uk
Find out how education works in Scotland – all the qualifications
listed and explained.

Special Educational   http://www.dfee.gov.uk/
Needs   sen/senhome.htm
The government's pages for parents of children with special needs.
The site provides information, links and online resources covering
resource material, teaching methods and advice.

___

Schools

Schools Net   http://www.isuk.org.uk
Search for the perfect independent schools around the UK.

Schools Register	http://www.schools-register.co.uk
Find your local school.

UpMyStreet.com	http://www.upmystreet.co.uk
For your local school, its results and catchment area, just type in your postcode – often very slow, but it's worth persevering.

Further and Higher Education

Floodlight	http://www.floodlight.co.uk
Every evening and part-time course available in London is listed here, ready for your application form. If you want a UK-wide picture, look at the On Course site.

National Union of Students	http://www.nus.org.uk
Working for more fun and a better deal for students.

On Course	http://www.oncourse.co.uk
Over 20,000 part-time and evening courses taking place across the whole of the UK – a far broader range than the London-bound Floodlight site.

Postgraduate and	http://www.merlinfalcon.
MBA Courses	co.uk
Follow up your degree with a post-graduate course – these guides will help you choose the perfect MBA, taught postgraduate courses and postgraduate research opportunities.

Red Mole	http://www.redmole.co.uk
Essential guide for student life – mixing beer, music, money and, yes, study.

Student UK	http://www.studentuk.com
Your life as a student – guides to managing meagre cash reserves, studying, sport, films and life after the three-year gig.

Student World	http://www.student-world.co.uk
How to find a course that suits you. Everything's included from admissions to music, and job-hunting to shopping.

UCAS   http://www.ucas.ac.uk
Higher-ed courses and degrees on offer in universities around the
UK. Enter what you want to study and your qualifications to find
out what's available, then make enquiries before the results come
out and the stampede starts.

//EVENTS AND DAY TRIPS

The Internet is full of ideas for where to go and how to entertain
the whole family for a day. There are plenty of directories of great
day trips and diaries of local events, but few of the destinations
listed have their own sites. It's hard to convey the thrills of a roller
coaster or safari park on a computer screen, but those attractions
that have put the effort into their sites prove it's possible.

If a ticket's involved, try the online booking agents – they often
have tickets for sold-out events, concerts and gigs. However, the
main point of all these sites is to get the family out of the house for
the day, so surf quickly and get going.

Starting Points

Baby Directory   http://www.babydirectory.com
Masses of ideas of where to go with your baby or children under
five.

@UK   http://www.dedicate.co.uk/@uk/
Child-friendly events happening in your local area.

Families.co.uk   http://www.families.co.uk
Brilliant directory of places to go that'll happily welcome children.

KidsNET   http://www.kidsnet.co.uk
Things to do that'll keep the whole family happy.

Leisure-UK   http://www.leisure-uk.co.uk
Find a local lion or roller coaster in this directory of zoos, theme
parks and places to visit.

London Evening Standard   http://www.thisislondon.com
What's happening in and around London.

Day trips

Alton Towers   http://www.altontowers.com
Scare yourself silly on the wild rides at just about the biggest British theme park.

Bristol Zoo Gardens   http://www.bristolzoo.org.uk
Swim through the amazing virtual online aquarium.

Blackpool   http://www.blackpool.com
Trad Brit seaside hols.

Edinburgh Zoo   http://www.edinburghzoo.org.uk
Lions, tigers and lots of penguins in Scotland.

Tower of London   http://www.camelot-group.com/tower/
Lose your head.

Thorpe Park   http://www.thorpepark.co.uk
Wet through – water and fun from this theme park.

Warwick Castle   http://www.warwick-castle.co.uk
Hugely popular fortress.

West Midlands Safari Park   http://www.wmsp.co.uk
Meet the tigers face to face.

Tickets

Aloud   http://www.aloud.com
Tickets to any and every gig. Brilliant.

Concert Breaks   http://www.concertbreaks.com
Tickets for concerts in the UK and Europe wrapped up in a neat package with hotels and travel.

Lastminute   http://www.lastminute.com
Don't plan ahead and save a fortune. Great deals on top hotels, restaurants, concerts and flights.

SceneOne   http://www.sceneone.co.uk
Your local entertainment guide – provides listings for TV, theatre, music gigs, radio; find what you like then buy the ticket (or the book or video).

theatre-link   http://www.theatre-link.com
More than a whiff of greasepaint coming from this site – what's on, how it's done and who performed. Good international coverage plus tickets and availability.

Ticketmaster   http://www.ticketmaster.co.uk
Tickets for everything.

Tickets Online   http://www.tickets-online.co.uk
Tickets to music gigs, theatre and comedy shows.

Way Ahead Online   http://www.fortunecity.com/
Box Office   wayahead/
Find an event, book the ticket, then track it to your door.

What's on Stage   http://www.whatsonstage.com
Instantly order tickets to any theatrical performance.

//FILMS AND TV

Trivia is big on the net – and it doesn't get much more trivial than film and TV gossip.

The best place to start exploring is the mega movie site from the Internet Movie Database. It's got a stunning range of film reviews, links to film directors and profiles of the actors in each production. Every major film has its own website – again use the Internet Movie Database to find the site's address (though often it's easy to guess, as in www.starwars.com).

And if you're reasonably patient, you may be able to download a tiny clip of your favourite movie. You'll soon figure out that it's far easier to pop around to your local cinema or video shop. If you do tear yourself away from your computer to visit a cinema or watch TV, use Scoot to get listings and times for your local cinema and Popcorn for the latest TV schedules, wherever you are.

Starting Points

BBC   http://www.bbc.co.uk
Vast, high-quality site about its programmes, education, news – and, well, everything.

Odeon   http://www.odeon.co.uk
Preorder tickets for the flicks (use Scoot www.scoot.co.uk to see what the other cinemas are showing).

Popcorn   http://www.popcorn.co.uk
Light, fluffy and fun magazine covering the news and local listings for films and TV.

SceneOne   http://www.sceneone.co.uk
Local listings for TV, theatre, music gigs, radio; find what you like then buy a ticket or video.

The Internet Movie Database   http://www.imdb.com
Stunning, well-organised database of over 180,000 film titles; it's easy to search films according to title, actors, producers or directors, and then browse reviews, synopsis and background data on each and every one.

Toaster   http://www.toaster.co.uk
Every TV programme from every UK channel and satellite and cable supplier is listed here – but you'll have to get off the sofa to read it.

Yack!   http://www.yack.com
Live online celebrity interviews and chats are now commonplace,

but finding when and where they happen is hard work. Jump to this site for a list of who's talking when.

Programmes

Many of your favourite programmes now have their own websites – so why not have a look?

Big Breakfast	http://bigbreakfast.channel4.com
Blue Peter	http://www.bbc.co.uk/bluepeter/
Brookside	http://www.brookie.com
Coronation Street	http://www.coronationstreet.co.uk
EastEnders	http://www.bbc.co.uk/eastenders
MTV Online	http://www.mtv.com
Sesame Street	http://www.sesamestreet.com
Teletubbies	http://www.bbc.co.uk/education/teletubbies/
The X Files	http://www.thex-files.com
Top of the Pops	http://www.totp.beeb.com

Reviews and Info

Astrophile http://www.astrophile.com

Was she really in that film? Hundreds of celebrities are profiled with potted biographies, interviews, pictures and news. The flip-side Dead People Server (www.dpsinfo.com) site just tells you if the stars are dead or alive.

Empire http://www.empireonline.co.uk

Brilliant flick site that includes over 4,000 reviews and features, plus full film listings from Scoot.

Filmworld http://www.filmworld.co.uk

Best for film festivals and obscure flicks; there are heaps of reviews – plus listings from Scoot – and if you like the review you can buy the video.

MovieGuru http://www.movieguru.com

Give the world the benefit of your critical notes on a new film. They'll be posted beside professional reviews and a mass of background info, archives and news on the film.

MovieReview http://www.cinema.pgh.pa.us/
QueryEngine movie/reviews/

Sparse design hides a massive database of reviews of movies – type in a movie title then follow the links.

Scene One Soaps http://www.sceneone.co.uk/s1/tv/

What's up in the Square, the Farm and the Street.

Gossip

Ain't It Cool News http://www.aint-it-cool-news.com

Probably the most influential Hollywood gossip site provided by a very well-informed amateur. Avoid it when LA wakes up – it's almost impossible to log on as film execs check whether they still have a job.

Beeb http://www.beeb.com

Chat, discussion, news and gossip about BBC TV and radio programmes but less impressive and informative than bbc.co.uk.

Cinescape Online http://www.cinescape.com

Keep up with the film industry news and gossip. A manageable site that's not as comprehensive as HollywoodReporter but it's free and bags good quotes from the stars.

E! http://www.eonline.com

Glitzy home of news, gossip and chat; lots of 'entertainment' personality stories with good photos and fun stories.

Mr Showbiz http://mrshowbiz.go.com

Comprehensive virtual reporter passes on the gossip on film and music celebs.

Cinemas and Broadcasts

AFI OnLine Cinema   http://www.afionline.org

Play it, Sam, play it – virtual cinema that screens classic Hollywood films.

Alternative Entertainment Network   http://www.aentv.com

A TV station and features magazine rolled into one. You can watch a range of classic films and TV programmes or read the 'making of' type of features.

broadcast.com   http://www.broadcast.com

Free live broadcasts of TV, radio and interviews. No special hardware is required: just connect and select the channel you want to watch.

KCTU TV   http://www.kctu.com

There's no escape from 24-hour live TV hell. This site broadcasts news, features, old episodes of Baywatch and other essential viewing.

Movie List   http://www.movie-list.com

Spend ten minutes downloading a fifteen-second preview of your favourite movie, then never bother again.

My Movies   http://www.mymovies.net

Cool design with zappy animation lets you see new-release trailers in a real-looking cinema setting, then check local cinema listings (via Scoot) to see where it's screened near you.

Buying Videos and DVD

101cd.com   http://www.101cd.com

A great range of CDs, videos, DVDs and computer games – plus books, all at discount prices. Includes reviews and staff recommendations.

Black Star   http://www.blackstar.co.uk

Vast range, discount prices, free delivery – together with reviews, news and plenty of special offers. Plenty of nice touches, like the hyperlinked cast list – and these are cross-referenced to help you find all the films with that star.

DVDnet http://www.dvdnet.co.uk
Very strong on news and reviews, with a very good selection of well-priced DVDs. The info for each title is complete and the descriptions good. You can write your own reviews, but the entries are not hyperlinked. You can also buy the hardware online – plenty of special offers.

DVDstreet http://www.dvdstreet.infront.co.uk
Impressive store selling DVDs only. Very easy to navigate, great biogs and hyperlinks, lots of news and reviews – free delivery and discounts make this a fab site.

Fat Sam's http://www.fatsam.co.uk
Fat Sam's currently offers over 200,000 different products available in the following categories: books, video tapes, audio CDs. The clear presentation of this site makes it easy to use. A good selection of special offers available.

Film World http://www.filmworld.co.uk
From Tim Roth to Eric von Stroheim. Great place for film enthusiasts – stocks an excellent range of independent, world and art films on video and DVD.

VCI http://www.vci.co.uk
Particularly good on TV shows on video, but with a modest selection of TV films plus books and music from this UK publisher and distributor.

All about films

Drew's Script-O-Rama http://www.script-o-rama.com
The mysterious Drew has gathered hundreds of original scripts that aspiring screenwriters can download and study – from *Alien* through to *A Clockwork Orange*.

James Bond   http://www.jamesbond.com

Not the retro archives of guns and girls you probably expected. Instead, a good-looking promo site for the new 007 film, with interviews, clips and news.

MovieTunes   http://www.movietunes.com

Composers and titles and the occasional clip of the great movie themes.

Oscars   http://www.oscars.org

All the news, history and glamour from the official site for the yearly Oscar awards – from the Academy of Motion Picture Arts and Sciences.

Star Wars   http://www.theforce.net

The unofficial – and much better for it – site about Luke and his adventures with a lightsaber. Great if you want to discuss Jabba the Hut's weight problem or just catch up on the gossip. The official site at www.starwars.com is very slick but mostly trumpets the latest release.

//FUN AND COMICS

Corny jokes, age-old punchlines and the latest comics are scattered all over the web. There are vast databases of jokes, each one rated and categorised, with some of the best gags and top lines from the classic acts like Groucho Marx and the Pythons.

More fun are the comics and comic-strip stories that are republished on to the web. Get a daily dose of Garfield, Snoopy or any of the major, syndicated characters.

Starting Point

Funny   http://www.funny.co.uk

If it isn't funny, it's not here – that's official. A directory of comedy sites on the web.

Jokes

KidsJokes.com   http://www.kidsjokes.com
Masses of jokes, riddles and 'knock-knocks' sent in by kids – as you'd expect, they're old, they're corny, but they're fun.

Jokes-4-You   http://www.jokes-4-you.com
Thousands of lines to raise an (often very weak) smile.

Other Amusing Websites

Comedy Central   http://www.comedycentral.com
Get your TV comedy fix with video clips from mainstream shows (including *South Park*) plus jokes and jolly screensavers.

Faces   http://www.corynet.com/faces/
Silly time-waster that's cheaper than laser surgery. Combine the various parts of celebrity faces to create truly ugly results.

Humor Database   http://www.humordatabase.com
Take thousands of jokes, rate them to make sure they don't offend and then store them by number. Boy, that sounds wild and wacky.

M&M's Network   http://www.m-ms.com
Cult animation from the sweet little guys who make little sweets.

Mr Bean   http://www.mrbean.co.uk
Gormless geek gets a website.

Cartoons and Comics

Garfield   http://www.garfield.com
Eat, sleep and ... well, eat and sleep with the fat ginger cat. Yikes, there's even a Garfield credit card.

Slylock Fox and Comics for Kids   http://www.slylockfox.com
Comic capers from Slylock, the detective fox, and his pals.

Cartoon Corner   http://www.cartooncorner.com
Fun place to learn how to draw cartoons, read a story or swap jokes.

Cartoon Network   http://www.cartoon-network.co.uk
Scooby Doo, where are you? He's here, with a mass of other silly cartoon characters.

Comics.com   http://www.unitedmedia.com/comics/
Official home of Dilbert and Snoopy.

Disney   http://www.disney.co.uk
Here's Mickey.

The Beano   http://www.beano.co.uk
Catch up with Dennis the Menace.

Peanuts   http://www.unitedmedia.com/comics/peanuts/
The official kennel for Snoopy – and poor Charlie Brown too.

Warner Bros.   http://www.kids.warnerbros.com
Bugs, Tweetie and the Animaniacs run riot.

//GAMES

Computer games. Some of the biggest time wasters known to children of all ages. They fall into two categories. There are nice, simple, traditional games such as chess, bridge, Scrabble and so on, which are harmless enough. Then there's multiuser Internet gaming, an absurdly addictive bug that can end in your total withdrawal from society.

It's mostly teenage boys – with their love of shoot-'em-up-style adventures – that dominate Internet gaming and there are hundreds of sites catering to the blood-and-gore enthusiasts. But parents should check to see how much time is spent in gaming sites and how much in homework centres – see page 26 for ways to limit access and, for extreme addicts, an Internet agreement for both sides.

Starting Points

Virtual Arcade 1.0   http://www.thearcade.com

Six rooms filled with online arcade games that link to other games' sites on the web.

Yahoo! Games   http://play.yahoo.com

The big Y lets you play over a dozen classic games quietly with a select band of ten thousand or more other users.

Online Adventure Games

Croft Times   http://www.cubeit.com/ctimes/

Astonishing amount of news about the curvy mega-babe Lara Croft and her adventures with snarling wolves in dark dungeons.

Doom   http://doomgate.gamers.org

Get the most from Doom in its stand-alone and multiplayer versions. A must-see site for doom players.

Game Post   http://www.gamepost.com

How much news can an online gamer read? Just about the most comprehensive coverage of news and reviews from the gaming front line.

Gaming Age   http://www.gaming-age.com

Busy site with news on forthcoming releases and interviews with game designers.

HEAT   http://www.heat.net

Arcade of online games, developed by SegaSoft, with dozens of titles like Quake and Star Wars. Free membership gives you limited access; paid membership provides access to the whole range.

Multi-Player Online Gaming   http://www.mpog.com

All the latest and favourite games for desktops and consoles, and a big section for online multiplayer games.

Official Lara Croft Fan Site http://www.eidos.co.uk/lara99/
Temple to the astonishingly built, streetwise cyber chick. See also
Croft Times (http://www.cubeit.com/ctimes/) for more (unofficial)
news about Lara than most can stomach.

The Vault Network http://www.vaultnetwork.com
Venture in to the dark underground centre full of news, features
and tips for RPG (role-playing game) enthusiasts.

Wireplay http://www.wireplay.co.uk
Originally a subscription-only service from BT, now a free and
fantastic place to play a good collection of online games.

Buying Computer Games

101cd.com http://www.101cd.com
Half-a-million games, books and video titles for sale. Add your own
review to any entry (rather like Amazon) or preorder forthcoming
releases.

CD Direct http://www.cddirect.co.uk
Good range for all platforms, plenty of reviews, promotions,
budget titles; and you can preorder forthcoming titles to make sure
you're the first to get a copy.

Game http://www.game-retail.co.uk
Total gaming overload with reviews, news, charts, product information – and all the games and accessories you could want.

Games Paradise http://www.gamesparadise.com
Great range for PCs and platforms – all at low prices. Includes
charts, reviews, and product details.

Nintendo Direct http://www.nintendodirect.co.uk
Wallow in the vast troughs of charts, news and reviews before
browsing heaving shelves stacked high with a great range of
Nintendo games.

Special Reserve http://www.reserve.co.uk
Just about the cheapest, widest range of computer games available. And, in case you're still deciding, there are reviews and gaming news.

Visions Online http://www.visionsonline.co.uk
Exchange a game you've done for a new game for PlayStation, Nintendo and Sega Saturn platforms.

Traditional Games Online

Action Man Island Command http://www.actionman.com
Kit out your action hero and play adventure games.

Chess Connection http://www.easynet.co.uk/worldchess/
My knight gets your pawn, check.

Cluemaster http://www.cluemaster.com
Fiendishly difficult crosswords and word puzzles.

Fun and Games http://www.blue-planet.com/fun/
An addictive Rubik's cube and retro Pac-man provide the highlights of this small range of Java games you can run from your browser.

Internet Park http://www.amo.qc.ca/indexPark.html
Bizarrely, 1,500 people have registered to play online, multiplayer versions of Scrabble.

MSN Gaming Zone http://www.zone.com
Impressive online games site. There are always thousands of people here playing interactive and multiuser games – including classics like backgammon and chess.

Nick Click http://www.coolcentral.com/nick/
Follow a private detective in this enjoyable online adventure game as he tries to solve clues in a Marlowe-inspired creation.

Riddler
http://www.riddler.com

A diverting selection of online word games, puzzles and cross-words – play by yourself or enter the online prize tournaments.

The Station
http://www.station.sony.com

Allow yourself plenty of free time when you visit to try out the great selection of online games including classics like chess and the multiplayer online game EverQuest.

Wild Card Games
http://www.wildcards.com

Nifty software that lets you play card games with any other Internet user; at the moment, the software is still free, but the developers may start charging at any time.

Traditional Games

Cluedo
http://www.cluedo.com

Who did it in the library with the candlestick?

Monopoly
http://www.monopoly.com

No online version to play, but you can catch up on the latest news – yes, there is some – check on local tournaments and gather hints on building your empire.

Scrabble
http://www.scrabble.com

The official home of the Scrabble word game. For more Scrabble words than you ever thought existed, try the SOWPODS site (http://www.ozemail.com.au/~rjackman/).

The Game Cabinet
http://www.gamecabinet.com

How to play it and rules to abide by for hundreds of (traditional and board) games.

The House Of Cards
http://thehouseofcards.com

Hear the card sharps shuffle as they practise the card games described in this encyclopedic site – from solitary solitaire to gambling with poker.

The London Chess Centre   http://www.chess.co.uk

Collection of books, videos, links to clubs and news on local tournaments. Save precious playing time and subscribe to their email e-zine.

//GARDENING

Gardening is the new craze for modern times, so it's fitting that it's also an unlikely web success story. You can plan your garden, search encyclopedias of plants and check that they suit your garden's location with the range of databases online. Then shop for shrubs, annuals or seeds to transform that muddy patch.

Before you escape from the children to the tranquillity of your vegetable patch, potter through the online gardening advice sites. There are centres for new or puzzled gardeners from the US and the UK, and chat sessions to discuss ideas with other gardeners. If you're having problems with your plants, ask an expert and find the answer.

Although the majority of the gardening sites are US-specific, choose a state that has a similar climate to the UK's and you can still work with the advice. The US is split into climate zones (USDA zones) – the Southern UK is equivalent to a USDA 8 and colder areas of the UK are equivalent to USDA 7.

Starting Point

Garden Centre   http://www.gardenworld.co.uk

Find your local suppliers and garden centres with this neat directory of the UK plus events and a few Q&As.

Plants

Birstall Garden Centre   http://www.birstall.co.uk

From sheds to stone slabs, seeds to roses, this garden centre has it all.

British Gardening Online　　　http://www.oxalis.co.uk
Friendly garden centre selling seeds, equipment and plants – plus plenty of information about gardens and garden centres open around the UK. Not as complete or slick as the US sites, but improving and much cheaper on shipping!

GardeningStore　　　http://www.gardeningstore.com
Official shop from the Royal Horticultural Society with a good range of books and a few (very few) plants.

Shrubs Direct　　　http://www.shrubsdirect.com
Boost your borders with a little something ordered from the 900 shrubs available from Cheshire.

Advice

Garden Solutions　　　http://www.gardensolutions.com
Ignore the advice about tropical plants – use the other thousands of Q&As in this US gardening site.

Garden Town　　　http://www.gardentown.com
Friendly, community feel to this US site. Plant reference material, advice and discussion groups.

Garden Web　　　http://www.gardenweb.com
The closest to leaning over the virtual fence for a natter. Lively discussion groups and good background reference material for all gardeners.

garden.com　　　http://www.garden.com
A friendly monster of a site. Helps you design your garden, gives advice, and has lots relevant to the UK.

Gardening Club　　　http://www.gardening-club.co.uk
UK-specific – which is rare – advice to help keep your garden blooming. But needs more in it and more for sale.

iGarden Magazine　　　http://www.igarden.co.uk
Practical garden magazine with tips and good advice for all gardeners.

RHS   http://www.rhs.org.uk
Beautiful design from the society for enthusiast gardeners. Unfortunately, it's weak on content and you'll find more practical advice elsewhere in this chapter.

Royal Botanic Gardens, Kew   http://www.rbgkew.org.uk
Sparse design, great content. Events, research and news from Kew and full access to its academic database of plants.

The Postcode Plants Database   http://fff.nhm.ac.uk/fff/
Dead begonias? Find out if your plants are compatible with your area. An essential first stop for all gardeners.

//HEALTH AND MEDICAL

There are some seriously useful medical websites on the Internet. If you are worried about a particular medical condition, or just want to know how to beat this year's flu, sites such as KidsHealth, DrKoop and IntelliHealth will offer good advice in plain English.

See the doctor!
Always ask to see your GP if you're seriously injured or ill. Advice from websites can be very good, but it's no substitute for a visit to the doctor.

Specialist sites provide impressive support for extreme or long-term medical problems. You'll get straightforward advice, the latest details on research and reassurance for partners and family plus the all-important chance to discuss problems – and their solutions – with others in the same position.

First aid is supplied from a rash of new sites – often via a charity or government bodies. Some include online video training for medical emergencies (such as mouth-to-mouth and heart resuscitation), but it's far better to attend a real rather than virtual course. More useful are general first-aid sites, such as First Aid, which explain how to deal with cuts, burns and splinters.

Starting Points

CPR Online   http://www.learn-cpr.com

That's Cardio-Pulmonary Resuscitation. Give mouth-to-mouth, help a heart-attack victim or save a choking child. Invaluable advice.

First Aid   http://firstaid.ie.eu.org

Top tips to deal with any injury or emergency.

General Health.   http://www.generalhealth.org

Masses of info on health issues.

Healthfinder   http://www.healthfinder.com

Thousands of links to help you explore health, medical and fitness sites.

KidsHealth.org   http://www.kidshealth.org

First stop for medical and health advice for your children.

Mental Health Net   http://mentalhelp.net/

Information on every form of mental health, from childhood eating disorders to recovery from abuse.

Medicine/Medical

Allergy Info   http://www.allergy-info.com

One of the slowest, most overused sites around – which is a shame since it's got everything you need to know about allergies.

Ask Dr Weil   http://www.drweil.com

Advice from an alternative-medicine expert, who will jump at the chance to provide a personalised vitamin-and-supplement list for your ailments.

British Diabetic Association   http://www.diabetes.org.uk

Quickly find specialist sites dealing with diabetes.

DrKoop   http://www.drkoop.com

Dumb name, great site. Everything about health, medicines and wellbeing.

drugstore.com http://www.drugstore.com
Virtual pharmacist provides almost every medical and health product you can imagine. Medical, beauty and nutritional information – you can even buy direct from the US. Partly owned by Amazon.com.

Intellihealth http://www.intellihealth.com
Answers almost all your medical questions, but geared to US enquiries.

Internet Mental Health http://www.mentalhealth.com
Packed with information about mental illness, including conditions, treatment and drugs. Don't expect a light read: the content is technical and aimed at professionals.

Mayo Clinic Health Oasis http://www.mayohealth.org
Rich on content and in design. Especially strong on cancer, Alzheimer's and heart disease.

Rare genetic diseases http://mcrcr2.med.nyu.edu/
in children murphp01/homenew.htm
Education, support and information sites for parents of children with genetic diseases.

The Allergy and Asthma Network http://www.aanma.org
Get the professionals' side of the story. For plain advice, try the Pfizer or Allergy-Info sites.

The On-line http://www.sig.net/~allergy/
Allergy Center welcome.html
Enterprising Texan allergy specialist sets out his stall, with live online chat sessions so you can talk about sniffles, rashes, wheezes and sneezes.

___
Good Advice
___

BeWELL.com http://www.bewell.com
Title explains all – for wide-ranging, sensible advice.

Boots   http://www.boots.co.uk

The high street hits the net with tips on beauty, health and medicines. But if you want to buy online you'll have to visit www.drugstore.com.

Center for Disease Control   http://www.
and Prevention   cdc.gov

All you never wanted to know about diseases around the world from this US government site. A handy chart warns travellers against current problems and epidemics.

DrugNet   http://www.drugnet.co.uk

Tells you the risks and problems of drug and alcohol abuse, then dishes out sensible advice – without the usual preaching or moralising.

Family Planning Association   http://www.fpa.org.uk

Prevent or plan that baby.

Mediconsult.com   http://www.mediconsult.com

Discuss your particular ailment with other sufferers – there are discussion boards for hundreds of different illnesses together with advice and support groups.

Meningitis Research Foundation   http://www.meningitis.org

Clear site leads you to the right resources by posing simple questions and providing the answers and support you might need.

OncoLink   http://www.oncolink.upenn.edu

Leading cancer-research centre delivers news, research and gently reassuring advice to any visitor.

Sleep Medicine   http://www.users.cloud9.net/
Home Page   ~thorpy/

Hardly the most exciting page designs – but perhaps that's the point of this site that's bursting with more information than you ever thought existed about sleep-related problems.

Royal National Institute for the Blind (RNIB)   http://www.rnib.org.uk

As you'd expect, very simply and clearly designed – and can be used with Braille readers, speech-synthesising web browsers or by any visitor with full vision.

Trashed   http://www.trashed.co.uk

Advice on drug abuse without the nannying.

Health and Exercise

Active For Life   http://www.active.org.uk

Get up, get active, get fit. Stop spending so much time peering into your computer screen, for a start.

Health Square   http://www.healthsquare.com

Helping women and families lead a healthier life.

Healthy Ideas   http://www.healthyideas.com

Masses of ideas for women trying to stay fit.

Women.com   http://www.women.com

Dedicated to women who want to know more about their health, fitness, children, career plans and illnesses.

Diet and Nutrition

Cyber Diet   http://www.cyberdiet.com

A sensible route to diet, exercise and nutrition advice with plenty of motivation.

Foodwatch   http://www.foodwatch.com.au

Get started on a healthier food regime – find out about the food you should or are about to eat.

HealthCalc   http://www.healthcalc.net

Go for a quick health check – calculate your body mass and find out your perfect mix of food types. If you want advice, it's a chargeable extra.

My Nutrition   http://www.mynutrition.co.uk

Step into the cool, calm clinic to find out about the perfect mix o'
healthy foods and vitamins.

//HOBBIES AND COLLECTING

Collecting, model making and genealogy top the list of hobbies or
the Internet. For many users, the Internet soon becomes their
overriding hobby, but you can use it to research a traditional hobby
chat to fellow enthusiasts or stock up on equipment or items fo'
your collection.

One of the major hobbies on the web is genealogy – plotting you'
family tree – which is particularly popular in America. For this, the
Internet seems ideal: unlimited access to parish records, telephone
directories, encyclopedias, census reports and family home pages
In fact, there's so much information, you'll need the help of one o'
the specialist genealogy sites to work out what's relevant and how
to use the information.

Starting Points

About.com   http://www.About.com/hobbies/

Hundreds of mini-sites covering different hobbies and crafts. Each
one's run by an enthusiast and is brimming with ideas, links and
encouragement.

Hobby World   http://www.hobbyworld.com

Hunt fossils, make models, throw a pot – how to do it and where
to find specialist sites on the web.

Yahoo!   http://www.yahoo.co.uk/
Hobbies   Recreation/Hobbies/

Yahoo's main directory page for hobbyists – listing thousands o'
sites on every pastime, collection and craft.

Collecting

Cameron's Matchbox Car Page http://userzweb.lightspeed.net/denney/cameron.htm

Astonishingly proficient four-year-old webmaster and his fine collection of Matchbox cars.

Coin News http://www.coin-news.com

Collect it, don't spend it.

Crown Agents Stamp Bureau http://www.casb.co.uk

Buy the latest UK stamps from the makers – the Crown.

Philatelic Resources http://www.execpc.com/~joeluft/resource.html

Vast directory of sites for stamp collectors.

Quasi Comprehensive Candy Bar Wrapper Image Archive http://www.bradkent.com/wrappers/

Obsessive collector of sweetie wrappers. Or try **http://jake.howlett.com/** for a smaller, but UK-centric view of the same ... erm, hobby.

Stanley Gibbons http://www.stangib.com

A rather uninspiring site from the big name in stamps.

Toy.co.uk http://www.toy.co.uk

Put a price on your collectable toys.

Dave's Wonderful World of Yo-Yos http://www.nmia.com/~whistler/yo-yos.html

Yo-yo heaven.

Junior Philatelists on the Internet http://www.ioa.com/~ggayland/junior/

Getting started with stamp collecting.

National Postal Museum http://www.si.edu/postal/

Stamp collecting on a vast scale – the Smithsonian Institute's vast postal museum.

Models

Big Little Railroad Shop   http://www.biglittle.com
From track to train sets, locos to stations.

Hobby Lobby International   http://www.hobby-lobby.com
Radio-controlled boats, planes and helicopters at low prices from
the US.

Tower Hobbies   http://www.towerhobbies.com
Your first place to call for anything to do with radio-controlled
models – thousands of items listed and shipped around the world.

Genealogy

Ancestry.com   http://www.ancestry.com
Search for your ancestors across 1,600 census and marriage
databases in the US – tantalises you with matching entries, then
demands payment.

family search   www.familysearch.org
Vast database set up by one Mormon church to help you track your
roots.

FamilyTreeMaker   http://www.familytreemaker.com
Awesome range of databases geared to families that migrated to
the USA.

Genealogy.com   http://www.genealogy.com
How to get started and where to look for a trail to your ancestors.

Hayden Genealogy   http://www.hayden.mcmail.com
Notes on over 950 family names compiled by an enthusiast
genealogist, Dennis Hayden. Also provides a route on to the
GenRing scheme to link genealogy sites.

Public Record Office   http://www.pro.gov.uk
Where all the births, deaths and marriages in the UK are recorded.

ociety of Genealogists   http://www.sog.org.uk
asic advice to get started tracing your family's roots.

K Genealogy   http://www.genuki.org.uk/big/
ast range of links to research and family sites to help you trace
our British ancestors.

Photography

t Your Leisure   www.shoppersuniverse.com
ood range of traditional and digital cameras and film – plus
uides to choosing and using the kit. Part of the vast Shopping
niverse mall.

ritish Journal of Photography   http://www.bjphoto.co.uk
ake better pictures, find an exhibition and catch up with the news.

uro Foto Centre   http://www.euro-foto.com
uge range of video, photographic, darkroom equipment,
ccessories and materials.

odak   http://www.kodak.com
lear guides to help you improve your photos.

ikon   http://www.nikon.com
ollow the online guide to take better snaps.

HOLIDAYS AND TRAVEL

dventure, advice and cheap tickets pretty much sum up this
ection. If you're after a cheap flight, take a quick sniff at the
fficial sites of the airlines to check seating plans and timetables,
en hurry on to the bucket shops. In this market for discounted air
ights, the customer is king. The web gives you instant access to
e same tools used by the high-street agents and you don't have
plod from shop to shop in your hunt for the perfect ticket.
stead, ask the online equivalents to compare prices for you.

Many people now use the Internet to book hotels, B&Bs or rented villas – whatever your budget. Instead of relying on printed brochures you can take a virtual stroll through the rooms, check the views to make sure there's no building site outside and the pinpoint the building on a local map.

Starting Points

Baby Directory   http://www.babydirectory.com
Masses of ideas of where to go with your baby or children under five.

Epicurious Travel   http://travel.epicurious.com
Great for ideas, daydreaming and planning but not so good for cheap tickets. Combines the style of Condé Nast's *Traveller* magazine with food, dining and online booking.

families.co.uk   http://www.families.co.uk
Where to go and what to do on rainy days, sunny days or holidays

Family Travel Files   http://www.thefamilytravelfiles.com
Where to go on hols and how to survive family life when you're there – lots on the USA, but also covers the rest of the world.

Kids Travel   http://pathfinder.com/travel/klutz
Survival tips when travelling anywhere in the world with you children.

MSN Expedia   http://www.expedia.msn.co.uk
Microsoft lands in the UK. Everything you need to research destinations and book flights, hotels and cars instantly.

Tickets

A2bTravel   http://www.a2btravel.com
Vying for top slot as best UK travel agent site. Everything your local agent can provide and so very much more.

Bargain Holidays   http://www.bargainholidays.com

Jaunty fun in the sun at cut prices.

Biztravel.com   http://www.biztravel.com

Maximise your frequent-flyer points and make the most of your expense account trips. Great for business users, but not always the cheapest tickets.

Cheap Flights   http://www.cheapflights.com

Automatically scour over thirty agents to find the cheapest deal.

Eurostar   http://www.eurostar.com

Travel from the UK to France and Belgium made very easy.

Lastminute   http://www.lastminute.com

Don't plan ahead and save a fortune. Great deals on top hotels, restaurants, concerts and flights.

Student Travel   http://www.statravel.com

Cheap travel and plenty of advice for students.

The Train Line   http://www.thetrainline.co.uk

One part of train travel made easy – plan your route and buy a ticket online.

Thomas Cook   http://www.thomascook.co.uk

Holidays, flights, currency and last-minute bargains from the high-street agent.

Travel Select   http://www.checkin.co.uk

Simple, efficient travel agent.

Travelocity   http://www.travelocity.co.uk

Just about the biggest travel agent on the web. Gives you instant access to the same system that's used by the high-street travel agents.

Guides and Resources

1Ski   http://www.1ski.com

Where to ski and the best deals available for package deals.

Africa Guide http://www.africaguide.com
Great gap-year fodder. An excellent guide to the 51 countries in Africa, covering medical and travel advice, together with links to local attractions, businesses and sites.

Britannia http://www.britannia.com
Central directory of sites that will help you plan, book and enjoy travels around the UK.

Family Adventure http://www.
Travel Directory familyadventuretravel.com
Find your perfect family white-water-rafting/safari holiday in this US-based, but worldwide directory of adventure tour operators.

Family Camping http://www.execpc.com/~thomas/camp.htm
Fancy the idea of holiday under canvas? Tips, ideas and experiences from American families that did just that.

Family Travel http://family.go.com/Categories/Travel/
Where to go for your next family holiday. Slick presentation from this Disney site, with the emphasis on the USA.

Family Travel Forum http://www.familytravelforum.com
Lots of information and informed comment from experienced parents who travel with their children – mostly geared to the USA, but still useful.

Home Schooling http://www.infinet.com/
Daily Camping Page ~baugust/camping.html
Lots of lists of things to do and take when camping. Great cub-scout material with recipes, rations, canoeing, knot-tying and ways to survive. Unless you're travelling to the US, you can ignore the section on places to camp.

International Student http://www.
Travel Confederation istc.org
Students sign up and travel the world on cut-price tickets, staying in hotels at rock-bottom prices.

LondonTown.com http://www.londontown.com
Take a big red double-decker tour of London.

Lonely Planet http://www.lonelyplanet.co.uk
Guide books to almost every world destination for the independent traveller.

Maps Worldwide http://www.mapsworldwide.co.uk
Find your way around any city or country.

Railtrack http://www.railtrack.co.uk
Clean, simple, efficient and it works. Much better than nagging National Rail Enquiries, but you should probably do that too.

Rough Guides http://www.roughguides.com
Great guides to countries and cities for independent travellers on tight budgets.

Strolling.com http://www.strolling.com
Beat the blisters and relax as you watch online video tours of London, New York, Paris and Dublin.

The Complete Gap Year http://www.gapyear.co.uk
Tons of information, ideas and links for students planning a year out.

Travelmag http://www.travelmag.co.uk
Fascinating features and masses of ideas for hols and adventures.

UK Travel Guide http://www.ukguide.org
A guide for visitors to (and residents of) the United Kingdom.

Virtual Tourist http://www.vtourist.com
Concise guides to local transport and visitor information for an impressive range of cities and countries.

Accommodation

Eurocamp http://www.eurocamp.co.uk
Camping and mobile home sites in the UK and Europe.

Club Med http://www.clubmed.com
Top-grade, all-in hols for families (and singles and couples) around the world.

Holiday Rentals http://www.holiday-rentals.co.uk
Holiday homes to rent around the world.

Infotel http://www.infotel.co.uk
Where to stay in the UK – includes, unusually, guest houses, with prices, location and rating. Online booking is antique but adequate.

International Home Exchange http://www.homexchange.com
Swap your semi for a palace.

Leisure Planet http://www.leisureplanet.com
See the hotel before you book; a vast collection of over 50,000 hotels each with a mini slide show plus area guides.

Mark Warner http://www.markwarner.co.uk
Fabulous hols with families in mind.

The Great British http://www.
Bed and Breakfast kgp-publishing.co.uk
Switch from hotels to homes and save – a guide to the hundreds of B&Bs around the UK. Unfortunately, there are no ratings.

//HOME AND DIY

As your family grows – and grows up – you'll need to redecorate, extend or even move home to keep pace. DIY and lifestyle are covered in enthusiastic detail by thousands of specialist sites, and the Internet will probably change for ever the way you'll find your new house. In the US, which is a couple of steps ahead of the UK, you can carry out the entire process – from getting a loan to choosing, visiting and buying a new home – from your keyboard. Visit the MSN Home Advisor for a quick tour of the future.

Online DIY guides and magazine-style sites help you make the most of your home. The UK sites from the DIY superstores are hopeless.

Instead, visit the mega US sites like HomeTips and NaturalHandyman, where a friendly expert will explain in simple steps how to build a partition wall, lay patios or deal with plumbing. Again, the advice is US-specific, so watch out – plumbing regulations and electricity voltages, for example, are quite different across the pond.

Starting Point

HomeTips   http://www.hometips.com
How to make and fix your home. Clear illustrations and step-by-step instructions hand-hold any novice DIY enthusiast. Also worth trying is the rival Natural Handyman site: http://www. naturalhandyman.com/.

DIY

B&Q   http://www.diy.co.uk
How to tackle DIY and where to buy the material. Plenty of online guides, but not up to the US mega sites.

Homebase   http://www.homebase.co.uk
Cool multimedia effects, but minimal content to tempt you back to the DIY superstore.

Buying a Home

Asserta   http://www.asserta.com
Almost every local estate agent's listings included to provide national coverage.

CyberHomes   http://www.cyberhomes.co.uk
Lease running out? Start looking for a new rental here.

Latitudes French Property   http://www.latitudes.co.uk
C'est formidable! Over 3,000 homes for sale in France.

MSN HomeAdvisor   http://homeadvisor.msn.com
One day, it'll all work this way. Stylish solution to finding a home and loan in the US.

PropertyFinder　　　　　　http://www.propertyfinder.co.uk
Database of national property on offer.

Property Sight　　　　　　http://www.property-sight.co.uk
Best range of homes for sale in the UK. Local agents keep the 7,000 listings up to date.

PropertyLive　　　　　　http://www.propertylive.co.uk
Plenty of advice to reduce the stress of moving once you've bought a house from the lists of property online.

In Your Home

Better Homes and Gardens　　　　　http://www.bhglive.com
Learn how to be the very model of an American suburban housewife.

Furniture Wizard　　　　　http://www.furniturewizard.com
How to remove the stain little Natasha's bottle left on your Chippendale.

HomeArts　　　　　　http://homearts.com
Coffee-morning worries. Living, lifestyle and women's mags provide plenty of advice for home and garden.

Lifestyle.UK　　　　　　http://www.lifestyle.co.uk
A list of all the sites you'll need to change your lifestyle. A good place to start browsing.

UpMyStreet.com　　　　　http://www.upmystreet.co.uk
How much is your house worth? More important, how about the Joneses' place at number 32? Ground-breaking site that catalogues house sales by postcode and provides all your local school and government information – often very slow, but persevere.

World of Interiors　　　　　http://www.the
Design Studio　　　　　designstudio.com
Avoid colour clashes – co-ordinate your curtains and chairs with this database of fabric and wallpaper samples and suppliers from the famous glossy mag.

//HOMEWORK AND EXAMS

Some sites mimic a real-life school and provide intensive additional tutoring for children who may need a little extra help with a subject. However, for many children, the problem is a lack of enthusiasm rather than ability. Just using the Internet to browse sites about their hated subject will make it more interesting. Can't stand French? Try conjugating online for a change or plug in your speakers and get started with correct pronunciation.

Once you have started to use the Internet for homework, help with teaching plans and advice or swotting up ready for a dreaded exam, you'll find it's impossible to do without it. But there's just one problem: it takes willpower to stick to the subject-specific sites and not start surfing off to comics, music or chat.

Starting Points

A-levels http://www.a-levels.co.uk
Directory of sites that'll help with any A-level subject.

BBC Education Homepage http://www.bbc.co.uk/education/
Auntie's clear and informative site should be your first stop for anything to do with education; provides sections for every level of education and a web guide to useful sites.

Channel 4 Schools Homepage http://schools.channel4.com
Impressive range of interactive learning material, for all children from infant to secondary level.

Educate Online http://www.educate.co.uk
Vast, if hard-to-navigate, directory of educational websites.

GCSE Bitesize Revision – http://db.bbc.co.uk/
BBC Education education-bitesize/pkg_main.p_home
The BBC wins again with these quick guides to revision on all the key subject areas plus guides and tests to make sure you're up to scratch before you sit the dreaded exams.

Homeworkline   http://www.bjpinchbeck.com
One teenager's mammoth collection of sites that'll help with homework.

School Zone   http://www.schoolzone.co.uk
A vast mass of 30,000 links to education sites, lesson plans, homework help and libraries.

Teen Hoopla   http://www.ala.org/teenhoopla/
Help for teenagers stuck with homework – a good selection of resources arranged by subject; but you'll get distracted by the teen-zines on sports, arts and comics.

ThinkQuest   http://library.advanced.org
Tutorials to help you in all the major subjects – very useful, but it's hard to find your way around.

Topmarks Education   http://www.topmarks.co.uk
Vast directory of educational sites, organised by subject and age range – the first place to find help with any homework or exam.

Online Lessons

Anglia Campus   http://www.angliacampus.com
A new amalgam of the old BT CampusWorld and Anglia Interactive sites that charges a subscription but has plenty of resources and lessons for home and school study on the national curriculum.

The Virtual School   http://www.virtualschool.co.uk
Quick, swot up on any GCSE or A-level subject online. For around £60 you'll get five weeks of tuition by email or chat session.

Infant School Subjects

Animabets   http://animabets.com
Let a gang of animals help teach your under-tens about a whole range of subjects.

Funbrain   http://www.funbrain.com
Improve numeracy and literacy for kids of all ages.

Funschool.com   http://www.funschool.com
Packed with educational games and activities to help teach youngsters the basics, but spoiled by banner ads.

Haring Kids   http://www.haringkids.com
Masses of activities and games to try to get children involved in the arts.

KidsCarnival   http://www.kidscarnival.com
Games to teach the time, numbers and letters; shame about the abundant commercials.

Kids' Summer Clubhouse   http://www.eduplace.com/kids/
Get the grey cells working over the summer – enter a reading challenge or try out brain-teasers.

Knowble   http://www.knowble.com
Have fun learning. Find out about all kinds of stuff with the help of cartoon guides.

Learning Garden –   http://learningedge.sympatico.ca/
CyberRecess   recess/cr.html
Online games to help with words, science and maths.

Letsfindout.com   http://www.letsfindout.com
Solve homework puzzlers with this multimedia encyclopedia aimed at children.

Literacy materials   http://www.standards.
and tools   dfee.gov.uk/literacy
The official word on the government's literacy hour – plus resources to help improve literacy.

Look, Learn and Do   http://www.looklearnanddo.com
History and science projects, stories and games – and even a teacher to answer your questions.

World Book Encyclopedia   http://www.worldbook.com/
Just For Kids   fun/jfk/html/jfk.htm
Read a story, improve your maths or find out about plants and animals with the help of this encyclopedia.

Zeeks.com   http://www.zeeks.com
Heaps of games that sneak up and teach you things, helped along with jokes, music and fun. Or talk to other kids with the chat rooms and your own email address. Marred by banner advertising – though you can pay to have an ad-free experience.

Zoom School   http://www.zoomschool.com
Virtual infant school that'll help teach the basics of geography, science, biology and arts.

Junior and Senior School Subjects

English

GCSE Answers   http://www.gcse.com
Past papers, sample tests and lots of help with revision; but just for maths and English.

Language Arts   http://www.mcdougallittell.com
Potted study aids to the main works of literature used in the US and the UK – these aren't full guides, but useful summaries with plenty of notes to help your revision.

Reflections Poetry   http://www.crocker.com/~lwm/
Enjoyable site that provides text and, in some cases, audio files with readings of classic poems.

The International Library of Poetry   http://www.poetry.com
A comprehensive collection of links to poetry sites plus news, reviews and discussion boards.

The Internet Public Library   http://www.ipl.org
Stroll through the aisles, pick up your favourite book and download

the full text for free. Great when you're studying a writer or chasing through their biographies.

The Literary   http://www.people.virginia.edu/
Web   ~jbh/litweb.html
Great writing is just a link away with this comprehensive listing of hundreds of literary sites, neatly organised in a simple layout.

The On-Line Books Page   http://www.cs.cmu.edu/books.html
From Austen to Zola, you can download the complete texts of over 9,000 books for free.

Winners of the Nobel   http://nobelprizes.com/
Prize in Literature   nobel/literature/
Who won the top literary prize? A mass of related links about that writer and their works.

Word Wizard   http://www.wordwizard.com
Explains the origins of words and phrases, new words and modern slang.

Classics

Latin   http://latin.about.com
Browse translations or ask the expert about your Latin homework.

Online Medieval and   http://sunsite.berkeley.edu/
Classical Library   OMACL/
Small, select range of the complete texts of some of the most influential early writers such as Chaucer. Great for students, academics and anyone bored by modern fiction.

Geography

Discovery Online   http://www.discovery.com
Start exploring the natural world – features on animals, explorers, wild places, and amazing facts.

Dundee Satellite   http://www.sat.
Receiving Station   dundee.ac.uk
Get an aerial view of the UK and the world.

Kids @   http://www.
nationalgeographic.com   nationalgeographic.com/kids/
All about countries, their history and discovery.

TerraServer   http://terraserver.microsoft.com
Satellite images of the world – zoom in to the towns and cities covered to get a street-level view.

The Fossil Company   http://www.fossil-company.com
All you need to know about those ancient skeletons in rocks.

History

Britannia History   http://www.britannia.com/history/
What happened and who ruled in the UK.

History Channel   http://www.thehistorychannel.com
Very readable articles that help make history more interesting.

History Fix   http://www.bbc.co.uk/knowledge/historyfix/
How to do your own historical research for your next project.

Junior Parliament   http://www.3t.co.uk/parliament/junior/
A good stab at making politics interesting for kids.

Viking Network   http://viking.no
Get to know the Vikings.

Egypt Fun Guide   http://www.seaworld.org/Egypt/egypt.html
Create your own cartouche and find out about mummies.

Languages

ALF: Interactive   http://ottawa.ambafrance
French Course   .org/ALF/

La plume de ma tante brought up to date with this written and spoken, basic French course.

Duden online   http://www.duden.bifab.de
Online versions of the respected Duden grammar and vocabulary courses – but you'll need to understand some German to navigate the site (or try the AltaVista – http://www.altavista.com – web-page translation service).

Little Explorers   http://www.littleexplorers.
Languages   com/languages/
Clear, illustrated first bilingual dictionary (in a range of languages) that's great for homework.

TravelLang   http://www.travlang.com
Online lessons start you off in fifty languages, with phrases, words, dictionaries and revision aids.

Mathematics

Calculator   http://www.calculator.com
Thousands of online gizmos to help calculate things.

GCSE Answers   http://www.gcse.com
Past papers, sample tests and lots of help with revision; but just for maths and English.

MathsNet   http://www.anglia.co.uk/education/mathsnet/
Helping kids get to grips with numbers with interactive testing and teaching material.

Megaconvertor   http://www.megaconvertor.com
Convert just about any measurement to something else.

The Constants and Equations Pages   http://tcaep.co.uk
All the equations, constants, resources and information you need for maths and sciences.

Sciences

ArchNet   http://archnet.uconn.edu
Dig up gems from this library of online archaeology resources.

Biology   http://websites.ntl.com/
website   ~webwise/spinneret/index.htm
You can't dissect a frog, but there's everything else for GCSE-leve
biology.

Dinosauria   http://www.dinosauria.com
Prehistoric beasts in all their glory. Particularly popular with little
boys still dreaming of *Jurassic Park*.

Discover Magazine   http://www.discover.com
Science and technology in palatable, reader-friendly features.

Earth and   http://www.fourmilab.ch/
Moon Viewer   earthview/vplanet.html
Real pictures of Earth and the moon; use the nifty navigators to
change your position and watch the shadows move.

How Stuff Works   http://www.howstuffworks.com
Great site for kids (and parents) – it does just what it says: from
engines to refrigerators, batteries to rockets.

Science Learning Network   http://www.sln.org
How the world works – a dozen museums, forums and features to
encourage children to investigate.

Science Library   http://www.luc.edu/libraries/science/
Dust down the test tubes and Bunsen burners as you browse this
well-stocked science library, which provides loads of resources for
all science disciplines (junior school and up).

SciTech Daily   http://www.scitechdaily.com
Daily news reporting advances in science. Plenty of links make this
a good place to start on homework projects.

The Last Word http://www.last-word.com

Answers to your questions from the team at *New Scientist*. So why is the sky blue? Great for children with homework or flummoxed parents.

The Sciences http://library.advanced.org/
Explorer 11771/english/hi/

Help for anyone tackling maths, physics, biology or chemistry. Part of the excellent ThinkQuest site – though it's hard to find from the main site's home page.

The Why Files http://whyfiles.news.wisc.edu

Clear explanations of the science behind news stories and events – from mad-cow disease to genetics.

KIDS ONLY

Kids need their own space to hang out, chat with friends or just kick back. The Internet provides masses of clubs that are free to join and great fun, with news on sport, music, fashion, trends, games and chat rooms.

Most club sites are intended for kids who are eight and older, but parents should check the site first to make sure it's at a suitable level. Once signed in, you can leave your children free to romp in the games rooms or huddle in the chat rooms. The sites are usually monitored by the organisers to ensure that there's nothing unpleasant going on. One commercial reality is that the most impressive, and therefore expensive, sites will probably sport advertising banners.

Oddly, there are sites for both boys and girls and sites just for girls, but so far there's nothing just for boys – although, in cyberspace as in life, boys do tend to take over the mixed clubs. The girls-only clubs are great for gossip, advice on health, beauty and personal problems that are too embarrassing to discuss with parents.

They're also just about the only place that are free of the shoot-'em-up games so loved by many boys.

Starting Points

Headbone Zone   http://www.headbone.com
Self-styled wackiness but covers all the big topics for kids. There are sections on love, advice, sports, cartoons, email, shopping and jokes – but too many commercial sponsors tempting little people.

Scoutbase UK   http://www.scoutbase.org.uk
It's hardly cool, but it's fun – everything for scouts, beavers, and guides. Or try the official worldwide HQ, which is worthy, but not as interesting (http://www.scout.org).

World Kid's Network   http://www.worldkids.net
Vast collection of resources for children to chat, play games, read a story or ask about homework problems.

Places to Hang Out

ACEkids   http://www.acekids.com
Dull-looking site that's best for its links to kids' homepages and its co-operative of bright children helping others with homework.

Bonus.com   http://www.bonus.com
Places to chat, stuff to do, music and fun – a safe, very controlled (its own browser takes over) environment. Luckily, the content's great fun.

Cyberkids   http://www.cyberkids.com
E-zines, stories, music, reviews, chat sessions, interviews and cartoons in a safe, monitored environment.

FreeZone   http://freezone.com
Let your 10–14-year-olds romp around this safe environment with chat pages, discussion groups, advice and games.

KidsCom   http://www.kidscom.com

A friendly place for kids to start exploring, exchange messages, play games and send e-postcards. Less wacky than Headbone Zone but without the protection of Bonus.com.

Stickerworld   http://www.stickerworld.org

A safe, monitored place for pre-teens to trade electronic stickers, chat and have fun (from the people who produce *Sesame Street*).

Teen Hoopla   http://www.ala.org/teenhoopla/

Supposedly here to help teenagers stuck with homework; but they'll get distracted by the teen-zines on sports, arts and comics.

Teen-Net   http://www.teen-net.com

Dating, music, films, chat, sports and fashion. Phew.

Just for Girls

A Girl's World Online Clubhouse   http://www.agirlsworld.com

Nail varnish, advice, chat and empowerment (terrifying for parents!) for 7–17-year-olds – typical features tell you how to turn babysitting into a money-making operation.

American Girl   http://www.americangirl.com

Write secret coded emails, read about adventures, get advice and buy clothes – fun for sensible, all-American girls or those who would like to be.

Girl Tech   http://www.girltech.com

For gizmo- or web-crazed girls. Hi-tech guides, chat, sports and profiles of inspirational women.

Girl Power!   http://www.health.org/gpower/

Health-and-fitness advice, help on self-image, and sports for 9–14-year-olds.

Just for Girls   http://www.girlscouts.org/girls/
Great fun for inquisitive girls – the US Girl Scouts have piled in science, technology, environment, sports, careers and medical advice.

Purple Moon   http://www.purple-moon.com
Chat, create a web page and make friends. Perfect for girls aged 8–12 (who will need their parents' consent for some sections).

//MONEY

It's relatively easy to totally computerise your banking and investment details, but this is just one part of the money jungle. The Internet now helps improve your buying power with guides and comparison tools to help maximise savings and minimise bills. For example, Blay's Guides sort through the savings accounts on offer and will show you the best rates. If you're spending rather than saving, Car Quote and Screen Trade will hunt through insurance and mortgage offers to cut your payments, while MoneyNet will send you the best deals from credit-card companies.

Starting Points

Yahoo! Finance   http://finance.uk.yahoo.com
The mega-portal provides straight financial facts, news and figures.

InvestorWords   http://www.investorwords.com
Before you buy it, check you know what it means. Clear definitions to over 5,000 complex financial terms.

Stocks and Shares

Charles Schwab   http://www.schwab-worldwide.com
Buy, sell or research from the biggest online broker. Excellent resources, graphing and investment advice, but you'll need to register and deposit some cash first.

E*Trade http://www.etrade.co.uk
Online trading, research, advice and investor discussion pages.

interactive investor http://www.iii.co.uk
Free share, investment, pension and mortgage prices; provides historical values, graphs, news and research – but you'll need to go elsewhere for online dealing.

TrustNet Limited http://www.trustnet.co.uk
If you worry about unit and investment trusts rather than stocks and shares, here's where you'll find news and prices.

Advice

Blay's Guides http://www.blays.co.uk
Which savings account provides the best interest rates.

Financial Information Net Directory http://www.find.co.uk
As the title says, it's full of information about anything financial. Tells you what's available and how to invest.

FT Quicken – Personal Finance http://www.ftquicken.co.uk
Solid advice for the average financial consumer.

MoneyExtra http://www.moneyextra.com
Compare mortgages, credit cards, savings accounts, pensions, life assurance – then pick the best.

Money World http://www.moneyworld.co.uk
An impressively complete site that tries to cover all aspects of personal finance – and generally succeeds.

Moneynet http://www.moneynet.co.uk
Choose the perfect credit card or mortgage. Fill in a form and you'll be sent details of dozens of deals.

MoneyWeb http://www.moneyweb.co.uk
Good, free information on how and where to invest.

The Motley Fool UK http://fool.co.uk

These are the guys who helped start the whole online share mania, now in the UK. Clear reports and information to debunk the myths and prove that professionals aren't always right. Very active discussion groups let you natter about your top tips.

The Treasury http://www.hm-treasury.gov.uk

What's happening to tax and interest rates? Find out from the official UK government site on budgets and economic indicators.

This Is Money http://www.thisismoney.com

The inescapable truth about life, death and taxes. Great for money newbies – with clear but realistic news and features.

Insurance

Car Quote http://www.carquote.co.uk

Fill in the online forms and you'll get car insurance quotes emailed or posted to you from a range of suppliers.

Home Quote UK http://home.quote.co.uk

Fill in your details and you'll get house-insurance quotes from half a dozen companies.

Screen Trade http://www.screentrade.co.uk

Reduce your insurance by comparing umpteen different suppliers – for car, house and travel.

//MUSEUMS AND GALLERIES

View the best works from the greatest artists without leaving your home. The Internet lets you visit the world's galleries, museums and private collections, and even have access to the historical and scientific notes and data hidden from the public.

World galleries are switching on the Internet as a way of displaying current shows and archive material to a wider audience. Visit the MoMA in New York, the sleek Louvre in Paris, J Paul Getty's museum on the West Coast or revel in the entire works of the Tate – online.

Starting Points

Art for Kids   http://artforkids.about.com
From finger-painting to piano lessons, this vast collection of links and reviews is an ideal starting point.

Art Guide   http://www.artguide.org
See what's on display in UK museums and galleries before you set off.

Art Planet   http://www.artplanet.com
Every fine-art site listed. Museums, artists, galleries, suppliers.

ArtLex – dictionary of visual art   http://www.artlex.com
Instant understanding – Press Ctrl-N to display a second browser window to keep this dictionary handy as you visit the other sites in this chapter!

WebMuseum   http://www.southern.net/wm/
The world's greatest artists brought together in one virtual warehouse. Perfect for students and classroom visits.

World Wide Arts Resources   http://wwar.com
Want art? Here's a vast mass of links to museums, artists, galleries and exhibitions. A great place to start exploring.

Artists

Claude Monet   http://www.claudemonet.com
Vincent Van Gogh   http://www.vangoghgallery.com
Picasso   http://www.club-internet.fr/picasso/
Leonardo da Vinci   http://www.webgod.net/leonardo/

Art Galleries

ArtMuseum.Net   http://www.artmuseum.net
Tackles a single exhibition very well – video walk-throughs and stunning pictures cover the subject in great detail. So far, van Gogh and American painters have been profiled.

Germanisches Nationalmuseum   http://www.gnm.de
One of the most impressive museums in the world housing art, sculpture, cultural, folk and design from prehistoric to contemporary.

Guggenheim   http://www.guggenheim.org
Skip among the six museums, marvel at the cool design, enjoy selected pictures, worry about the slipping deadlines on its project to create a virtual museum.

J Paul Getty Museum   http://www.getty.edu
Take a tour round the billionaire's beautiful house and art collection high above the Californian coast.

Louvre   http://mistral.culture.fr/louvre/louvrea.htm
Paris's palace of art, beautifully rendered. Pictures come first but – Mon Dieu! – the spelling.

Metropolitan Museum of Art   http://www.metmuseum.org
Save the airfare. Landmark New York monument displays its stunning collection of art and cultural treasures online.

MoMA   http://www.moma.org
Avoid the queues curling round to Fifth Avenue – the NY museum that's as famous as its exhibits puts on a great web show.

National Gallery   www.nationalgallery.org.uk
Tremendous collection of western European paintings displayed online with plenty of accompanying notes.

Tate Gallery   http://www.tate.org.uk
Every gallery should follow this example. View almost all the pictures in the Tate collection in London together with notes on the artist and subject. Brilliant.

Uffizi Gallery, Florence   http://www.uffizi.firenze.it
Virtual-reality tour of its fabulous masterpieces, including Botticelli's *Birth of Venus*.

Specialist Museums

Imperial War Museum   http://www.iwm.org.uk
Tanks for the memory. Tanks, trenches and the horrors of war.

Library of Congress   http://www.loc.gov
Everything that made America great. Huge site with historical, cultural and political material from the official US archives.

London Transport Museum   http://www.ltmuseum.co.uk
The history of the double-decker and tube.

Victoria and Albert Museum   www.vam.ac.uk
The building houses the finest collection of decorative arts in the world; from ceramics to costumes. Striking in design, but without the depth you would expect.

National Maritime Museum   http://www.nmm.ac.uk
A look back at man's constant battle with the sea.

National Postal Museum   http://www.si.edu/postal/
Stamp collecting on a vast scale – the Smithsonian Institute's vast US postal museum.

Science Museum   http://www.nmsi.ac.uk
Plenty of buttons to press and levers to pull at this playful site. Stacked high with guides, pictures and video clips of our scientific milestones.

Tech Museum   http://www.thetech.org
Last year's computers, gizmos and gadgets from the depths of the computer heartland, Silicon Valley.

The Natural History Museum   http://www.nhm.ac.uk
School coach trips are banished as you surf past the blue whale and dinosaurs. Visitors can pose questions to the experts in this enjoyable learning experience.

//MUSIC

Not only is the Internet full of people who want to share their enthusiasm for their favourite bands, but there are record companies' sites, magazines and official band websites galore. And if you're ready for a challenge you can learn to play a musical instrument or just download and listen to the latest hits. There are hundreds of sites devoted to classical music and individual composers as well as hip-hop, electronic and plenty of experimental stuff.

There are probably more sites writing about music than playing it. All the major bands have websites – often within their record company's site. But for a complete – if obsessive – view of your favourite band you'll have to turn to fanzines that include everything about the band and its lyrics. If you listen to your radio or a CD when you surf, try instead one of the hundreds of Internet radio broadcasters. There are channels for every musical taste.

The biggest challenge to the traditional music industry is the development of the MP3 (MPEG-3) standard. This allows anyone to store CD-quality stereo sound in a relatively small file (one minute of music takes up around 1Mb of disk space). Many people are copying normal CDs into MP3 format and making these copies available on the Internet. It's this illegal copying and free distribution that the music industry rightly sees as a threat.

Starting Points

All-Music Guide http://www.allmusic.com
A super-sized encyclopedia of pop, rock and classical reviews, biographies and discographies rolled into one. If you can tear yourself away, also try Worldwide Internet Music Resources (http://www.music.indiana.edu/music_resources/).

Ultimate Band List http://www.ubl.com
Obsessed with a band? Join its fan site. Everything to help the pop-crazed bopper get a fix.

Yahoo! Music　　　　　　　　http://rock.yahoo.com
Neat summary of what's happening in the rock and pop scene –
with live broadcast schedules, US charts and reviews.

Harmony Central　　　　　http://www.harmony-central.com
Vast directory of instrument-specific, band and music sites.

Music Education Launch Site　　　http://www.talentz.com
Great place to start exploring, with masses of music lessons, games
to teach theory and links to other music sites.

Great Pianists　　　　　http://www.philclas.polygram.
of the 20th Century　　　　nl/class/pihome/basis.htm
Neat biographies on a couple of hundred great pianists.

Instrument　　　　　　　http://www.si.umich.edu/
Encyclopedia　　　　　CHICO/MHN/ENCLPDIA.HTML
Bongos to piccolos, described and photographed in an
encyclopedic format that includes links to other useful sites.

Classical

Classical　　　　　　http://www.musdoc.com/classical/
Fine collection of articles, reviews and biographies of classical
composers and their works.

Classical Composers　　　　http://utopia.knoware.
Database　　　　　　　　nl/users/jsmeets/
Classic composers get the rock-star biography treatment, though
Classical Net is probably better for enthusiasts.

Classical Net　　　　　　http://www.classical.net
Biographies and recommended play lists put together by amateur
enthusiasts for enthusiasts.

Classic FM　　　　　http://www.classicfm.co.uk
Online version of the hugely successful radio station. Brings
classical music to the masses. Do we deserve this?

CD Megasites

The marketplace is dominated by vast warehouse-style shops selling hundreds of thousands of titles at low prices. The following mega sites provide a similarly huge range:

101cd.com	http://www.101cd.com
Amazon.co.uk	http://www.amazon.co.uk
Audiostreet	http://www.audiostreet.com
Borders	http://www.borders.com
CDNow	http://www.cdnow.com
CD Universe	http://www.cduniverse.com
Music Boulevard	http://www.musicblvd.com
IMVS	http://www.imvs.com.

Buying

Action Records   http://www.action-records.co.uk

Three unique points: one, they still sell vinyl; two, they also have a real shop; three, they also have their own music label. Sum – a great place to shop for indie and mainstream.

cdparadise   http://www.cdparadise.com

Cut-price CDs, videos, computer games and books. Features 'Brad', the virtual assistant who'll keep you informed of new CD releases. Part of the WH Smith empire.

GEMM   http://www.gemm.com

Track down hard-to-find CDs with a neat search tool that looks in all the new and second-hand online stores.

HMV   http://www.hmv.co.uk

High-street music store for mainstream soul, jazz, pop and classic CDs, DVDs and videos.

MDC Classic Music   http://www.mdcmusic.co.uk

Excellent selection of classical music CDs for sale.

Razorcuts http://www.razorcuts.com

Browse the site for tracks you want – from jazz to lounge, classic to disco – and create your own custom CD. Cool.

Tunes.com http://www.tunes.com

Vast CD shop that gathers reviews from the All Music Guide site and adds a million sound clips, news from *Rolling Stone*, thousands of video clips and several hundred thousand titles with reviews.

Downloading MP3s

Lycos http://mp3.lycos.com

Search engine gets an honourable mention here because it's about the best place to search for bootleg MP3 files to download and play.

MP3.com http://www.mp3.com

Plenty of news on copyright laws, the software you need to play back the files and a good range of new indie bands using MP3 to preview their sample tracks. Thousands of funky unknowns and a smattering of classical pieces, but no major artists.

MP3 World http://www.worldkey.com/mp3world/

Read the 'is this illegal?' box as you search the archive of MP3 music to download.

RioPort http://www.rioport.com

Advertising its eponymous neat, tiny, portable MP3 player, plus a whole mass of links where you'll find MP3 files.

Reviews and Magazines

Addicted To Noise http://www.addict.com

Sonic sonnets from some of the coolest tune-hacks in the US – monthly articles make this a great read.

Billboard http://www.billboard-online.com

The famous magazine keeps you up to date with news stories and

a few charts. For the full archives and all the charts, you'll have t
pay – unless you visit **http://rock.yahoo.com/**, where you'll see th
same listings, in full, for free.

Dotmusic   **http://www.dotmusic.con**
Pretty much the perfect mix of gossip, official news, preview
biogs and – to fund it all – sales of CDs.

MTV Online   **http://www.mtv.con**
Just like the TV show. Hundreds of bands, mini video clips an
preview tracks in a sharp new site.

music365   **http://www.music365.co.u**
Mostly mainstream pop and chart news, previews and feature
Great if you're into Cher or Michael Bolton, but for the alternativ
scene try NME or Addicted to Noise.

NME   **http://www.nme.con**
Serious rock'n'roll reviews and news from *New Musical Express*.

Rolling Stone   **http://www.rollingstone.con**
Just a sample of the classic interviews and photos. Shame, woul
be fantastic to have the lot.

SonicNet   **http://www.sonicnet.con**
Straight-talking guide to what's up in the music scene. Fror
Mariah Carey to the Chemical Brothers, this award-winning sit
does it all with style.

Top 3   **http://www.top3.ne**
Mad about pop music? Lyrics for 200 top pop songs, MP3 sample
and reviews. There's a strong bias towards US bands, but there's sti
a lot here.

Broadcasts

Capital Radio   **http://www.capitalfm.con**
London calling. Live broadcasts from Chris Tarrant and friends.

Live Concerts http://www.liveconcerts.com

Enjoy a gig from home.

NetRadio Network http://www.netradio.net

Over 120 free radio stations playing everything including 80s pop, rock and classical. A similar alternative is Spinner (www.spinner.com).

Virgin Radio http://www.virgin-radio.com

Classic tracks and new music broadcast live.

vTuner http://www.vtuner.com

Scan all the radio stations broadcasting live on the net. Search by style or country (the UK has 22 stations), then click and listen; each station is rated by quality of sound and speed of delivery.

Playing Instruments

Guitar Lessons http://www.guitarlessons.net

Finger-picking to chord work, learn it here.

Music Notes http://library.advanced.org/15413/

How to read music, the history of music and how instruments work.

Magic Music: http://library.advanced.org/
Online Piano Lessons 15060/data/lessons/

Easy lessons to help you learn to play the piano – includes sound files and theory tuition.

Piano net http://www.pianonet.com

Advice and lessons for wannabe piano players.

Playmusic http://www.playmusic.org

Fun guide to an orchestra and its instruments.

Sheet Music Direct http://www.sheetmusicdirect.com

Stuck for something to play? Buy and download sheet music for instant inspiration.

Buying Instruments

ABC Music   http://www.abcmusic.co.uk
Buy, sell or exchange your instrument at this Surrey-based shop.

Axemail   http://www.axe.music.co.uk
Guitars, amps and drum machines – plus a new section for sax
and flute.

Chappell of Bond Street   http://www.shopyell.co.uk/chappell
Wonderful collection of sheet music covering all styles and
instruments.

Churchill's Music   http://www.churchills-music.co.uk
Accessories for your synth or keyboard.

Don Mackrill's Music Stop   http://www.donmack.dircon.co.uk
Sax, brass and woodwind for sale.

Hobgoblin Music   http://www.hobgoblin.com
Bagpipes, flutes and citterns provide a backing for the huge range
of traditional, folk and Celtic instruments.

Internet Music Shop   http://www.musicsales.co.uk
Bright, friendly site filled with sheet music, tutoring systems
and videos.

Saxophone Rental Company   http://www.saxophones.co.uk
Rent a sax and learn to play.

Steinway and Sons   http://www.steinway.com
Waxes lyrical about the wonder of their own pianos, but includes
info for piano-mad children.

//NEWS

The Internet has proved its worth in delivering breaking news, and
not just via the web – Usenet newsgroups were the only way to
relay reports from civilians stuck inside recent war zones (such as

the conflict in Kosovo). Some of the biggest scandals have broken on the net – the world first read about the Monica Lewinsky affair on the Drudge Report website.

Children have their own news sites: the venerable, but wonderful, BBC Newsround site, and analysis from that of *Time* magazine. And to try to get kids interested in news per se, try Yak's Corner – it has the latest about stuff that's important to them, such as the price of sweets and brands of ice lollies.

Starting Points

BBC news http://news.bbc.co.uk

This is where much of the BBC's massive investment in online services has gone. Not as trendy as CNN, but the coverage is better. Includes features, in-depth analysis and even offers live video or audio news segments.

CNN http://www.cnn.com

Brimming with news, features and listings from around the world. It cost millions to develop this highly original site – and it was worth every cent, but the BBC has sharper European and UK coverage.

NewsPage http://www.newspage.com

World and business news on a grand scale. Reports gathered from over 600 magazines and newspapers, then sorted into 2,500 topics. If it's out there, it's in here – but it can be overwhelming.

Newsrack http://www.newsrack.com

Brilliant, simple idea done well. Links to (almost) every online newspaper and magazine site from around the world. If it's not here, try The Paperboy at http://www.thepaperboy.com/ or Worldwide News at http://www.worldwidenews.com/.

Newsround http://www.bbc.co.uk/newsround/

The only TV news programme your children will ever want to watch.

Time for Kids   http://pathfinder.com/TFK/
Time magazine's news and analysis – repackaged for children.

Yak's Corner   http://www.yakscorner.com
News and reviews that matter: children write what's coming up in toys, games and sweets.

Weather

BBC Weather   http://www.bbc.co.uk/weather/
What's happening with high- and low-pressure systems? Local and world weather by region plus shipping and pollen forecasts.

The Weather Channel   http://www.weather.com
The weather from around the world with three-day forecasts and mini satellite pictures. Factual but not as friendly as the BBC Weather site.

Yahoo! Weather   http://weather.yahoo.co.uk
With its five-day forecasts, Yahoo! predicts three days further ahead than rival Excite!

World News

Anorak   http://www.anorak.co.uk
Originally developed for busy share traders' screens to scan in their quiet moments, this site provides the quickest possible news fix condensing all the tabloid and broadsheet news and views into a mini commentary.

Crayon   http://www.crayon.net
Create your own newspaper from the subject sections, features and cartoons available. If you want email delivery, try InfoBeat.

InfoBeat   http://www.infobeat.com
Get a custom-made daily paper delivered free via email. Not a unique service, but this is the best for world coverage.

Press Association http://www.pa.press.net

Excellent coverage of news from around the world. Less US bias than CNN, and without the deluge provided by Reuters.

Reuters http://www.reuters.com

The biggest name in news gathering includes a terrifying news ticker that rolls on relentlessly, and an overwhelming quantity and quality of subject-specific news.

Specialist News

Africa News http://www.africanews.org

Gathers together news and features from over sixty sources covering all of the African states.

Arab World Online http://www.awo.net

Absolutely everything you need to know about the Arab world.

AsiaOne http://www.asia1.com.sg

Local, national and international news from Asia.

China News Digest http://www.cnd.org

General and business news from China together with the unique Chinese perspective on world news.

Drudge Report http://www.drudgereport.com

Millions of visitors stop for world news headlines, gossip and scandal – often exclusive – with features by Matt Drudge and top columnists from around the world.

Globe and Mail http://www.globeandmail.ca

Best-known Canadian newspaper from Toronto tells you what's happening in the vast landmass just north of the US.

InfoJump http://www.infojump.com

Find an e-zine that covers your interests and keep up to date.

London Student http://www.londonstudent.org.uk

Term-time fortnightly keeping students updated on the latest news.

Megastories   http://www.megastories.com
Analysis and comment on the news and breaking stories.

Russia Today   http://www.russiatoday.com
The news – in English – with plenty on Moscow politics.
Surprisingly Western in look and content.

Slate Magazine   http://www.slate.com
Enjoyable read with news and features – but hardly the wild child it
once was.

Sporting Life   http://www.sporting-life.com
Sports news. All of it.

SportLive   http://www.sportlive.net
News and results from the major sports – nicer to look at and
easier to read than the Sporting Life site but without the breadth
and depth.

Tass   http://www.tass.ru/english/
The Russian view on a particular story – described as a time line
through the day.

The Hindu   http://www.the-hindu.com
India's national newspaper. Full text (in English) with all the news,
business, sport, entertainment and classified ads.

The Hollywood Reporter   http://www.hollywoodreporter.com
Who's doing what with whom – and for how much.

The Jerusalem Post   http://www.jpost.co.il
News from Israel.

The Onion   http://www.theonion.com
Brilliant send-up of tabloid news and style. A must-have bookmark.

//PARENTING

Most parents muddle through the trials of bringing up baby,
learning by experience or the occasional tip from relatives; but go

online and you'll find an entire community of like-minded parents ready to share, advise and laugh at just the right times. How do you deal with toddler tantrums and teenage sulks, or just manage to juggle everything? All these sites provide advice, features, ideas and chat forums that won't make life any easier, but will reassure you that you're doing the right thing.

Help with Parenting

CyberMom http://www.cybermom.com
Mummy meets the Jetsons – tricks and advice to make Mummy's job easier. Very American, but very useful. Also worth trying is Moms Online (http://www.momsonline.com).

Family Internet http://www.familyinternet.com
Vast collection of everything you might want to know or do as a parent – from family finance to travel, health to TV.

Gingerbread http://www.gingerbread.org.uk
Support and advice for lone-parent families in the UK.

Happy Families http://www.happyfamilies.com
Family life with a smile.

I am your child http://www.iamyourchild.org
How your little toddler grows up and develops.

Kids Link http://sargon.mmu.ac.uk/welcome.htm
Support, advice and thousands of links to specialist sites for parents of children with special needs.

myFamily http://www.myfamily.com
Salvation for disjointed families. Create a family's meeting point and mantelpiece for photos, memos and calendar.

Parent Soup http://www.parentsoup.com
Relief for parents worried about their kids – or just plain worried. There's advice on education, health and even baby names.

Parenting   http://www.parenting-qa.com

Answers to all your questions about your children, their safety and education.

Parents Place   http://www.parentsplace.com

Family, health and happy children. Good advice and features with slick US presentation.

Practical Parenting   http://195.89.137.30/hp/AndyGill/

Jolly site for UK parents and carers, particularly good on child development and psychology.

Summer Fun   http://db.ok.bc.ca/summer/

Ideas for exhausted parents to entertain the small bouncy people. Includes recipes (for indoor and outdoor cooking methods) that have been submitted by other exhausted parents.

The Daily Parent   http://www.dailyparent.com

Family finance to midwives. This site's simple design neatly hides a vast mass of advice and subject-specific discussion groups on family life, health, education and pregnancy.

The Family Corner   http://www.thefamilycorner.com

Survive tantrums, work from home and plan stress-free travel – but best not at the same time.

The FUN place   http://www.thefunplace.com

Jolly American slant to life as a parent.

UK Mums Online   http://www.ukmums.co.uk

How to survive parenthood – if you've the energy to surf, you'll find advice on pregnancy, health, managing after the birth, and even how to change nappies.

Work at Home Moms   http://www.wahm.com

Want more on your plate? Masses of information, ideas and support for mums who want to juggle work and kids – without leaving home.

PETS, ANIMALS AND CONSERVATION

A pet is a child's best friend – it doesn't gossip, run away, beat you up or copy your homework. It does, however, need looking after and here the Internet helps out. There are plenty of sites full of advice to help you look after your furry, feathered or fishy friend. And, if you're thinking of getting a pet, a visit to the RSPCA site should be first on your list to get the real long-term view of ownership.

Instead of buying a pet, the environmentally minded child might want to be up with conservation or ecological issues. All the main organisations have websites and encourage sensible use of our existing natural resources, as well as information on how to volunteer for conservation groups in your area.

Starting Points

Environmental Education   http://www.eelink.net
Central directory for all things environmental.

NetVet and Electronic Zoo   http://netvet.wustl.edu
Vast directory of animal, conservation and veterinary websites –
choose an animal, then follow the links to learn more.

RSPCA   http://www.rspca.org.uk
Packed with good advice on looking after pets – and a cute little
animated fox.

Pets

AcmePet   http://www.acmepet.com
Advice, news, stories, polls, chat, and games for young pet
owners.

Animail   http://www.animail.co.uk
Lots of stuff to buy for your cat, dog or budgie in this well-stocked
shop.

Aquatics Warehouse   http://www.aquatics-warehouse.co.uk
Hundreds of goodies for your goldfish.

Battersea Dogs Home   http://www.dogshome.org
Hopeful dogs waiting for a new owner. Alternatively, persuade
your parents to support the charity via the Charity Credit Card
(http://www.charitycard.co.uk).

Cyber Pet   http://www.cyberpet.com
Start here for everything about cats and dogs.

Dog Problems   http://www.dogproblems.com
Secrets of a professional dog trainer – how to care for, train and
manage your best pal.

Equiworld   http://www.equiworld.net
Masses of information about horses and ponies and how to look
after and ride them.

geegees   http://www.geegees.co.uk
Enthusiastic advice and features for horse lovers in the UK.

Haynet   http://www.haynet.com
Slick American site for horse-mad surfers.

Horseweb   http://www.horseweb.co.uk
No-frills horsy site that lists horses and tack for sale.

Hotspot for Birds   http://www.multiscope.com/hotspot/
Great starting point that's just for bird lovers.

How To Love Your   http://www.
Dog Dot Com   howtoloveyourdog.com
Packed with friendly advice and stories to help your children look
after the new hound.

I Love My Pet.com   http://www.ilovemypet.com
Forget the mishap on the carpet, here's fun stuff to remind you
why you love the beastie.

Pet Cat   http://www.petcat.com

Tales from the litter tray. Kitty talk, how to look after your cat, diary of a cat and advice for young owners.

Pets Pyjamas   http://www.pets-pyjamas.co.uk

Information (and stuff for sale) for kids who want to look after their cat or dog.

Puppies and Dog Breeders   http://www.puppies.co.uk

Caring for little puppies. For those of you who want your own, here's advice and a search feature to find an approved breeder.

SitStay GoOut store   http://www.sitstay.com

Romp and jump and hunt and fetch accessories, equipment and goodies for your dog.

Wild Animals

Animal Information Database   http://www.seaworld.org

Tune in to dozens of webcams pointing at whales, sharks and less frightening animals.

RSPB   http://www.rspb.org.uk

Watch the puffins via the live webcams and learn masses about birds and wildlife conservation.

The Natural History Museum   http://www.nhm.ac.uk

School coach trips are banished as you surf past the blue whale and dinosaurs. Visitors can pose questions to the experts in this enjoyable learning experience.

The Yuckiest Site on the Internet   http://www.yucky.com

Perfect for (well, mostly) little boys: the gross goings-on of worms and other nasty natural things in this brilliantly conceived site.

Environment and Conservation

British Trust for Conservation Volunteers   http://www.btcv.org
Join up and help save a bit of grassland – practical conservation events for volunteers.

Endangered Species   http://www.eelink.net/EndSpp/
What's next? Endangered species and the work being done to help save them.

English Heritage   http://www.english-heritage.org.uk
Conserving not just old buildings, but also pastures, coastlines and natural beauty spots.

EnviroLink   http://www.envirolink.org
Join the community promoting environmental issues and clean, organic living.

Friends of the Earth   http://www.foe.co.uk
Helping to conserve and save the planet.

Greenpeace   http://www.greenpeace.org
Fighting for a better world without pollution or animal cruelty.

Living Almanac of Disasters   http://www.disasterium.com
Grim reminder of natural disasters – catalogued for every day of the year.

Natural History Book Service   http://www.nhbs.co.uk
Stock up your shelves with the latest on animal, environmental and conservation titles – plus news and resources.

Planet Ark   http://www.planetark.org
Environmental news direct from Reuters.

The Green Party   http://www.greenparty.org.uk
Political slant on environmental issues.

The National Trust   http://www.nationaltrust.uk.org
Working to preserve important British landmarks.

The Nature Conservancy　　　　http://www.tnc.org
Nature conservation made easy.

The Rainforest Action Network　　　http://www.ran.org
Help save the rainforests.

World Wide Fund for Nature　　　http://www.panda.org
Working hard to prevent destruction of forests, eco-climates and
the extinction of some species by man.

Young People's Trust　　　http://www.btinternet.
for the Environment　　　　com/~yptenc/
Get involved and help maintain and preserve our environment.

//REFERENCE

The Internet is a brilliant way to get help with tough general-
knowledge homework questions – but, for specific help with a
homework subject, use the online guides and revision help in the
homework section (see page 171).

Dictionaries make perfect fodder for an Internet site. In electronic
form they are quick and easy to search, you broaden your request
across hundreds of titles covering different languages and specialist
subjects – and it's free. Online encyclopedias work just as well and
provide invaluable help with homework or research. Answer local
queries with either the brilliant Scoot (based on the Yellow Pages
directory and listings) or UpMyStreet, which also has the audacity
to tell you the price of the houses in your street.

Starting Points

About.com　　　　http://www.about.com
Lots of mini-sites about hundreds of different subjects make this a
good place to look for anything.

Argus Clearinghouse　　　http://www.clearinghouse.net
Reference sites on the web rated and categorised. Dull but ever
so useful.

Discovery Online –   http://books.discovery.com/
Book Talk   booktalk.html
Turns the tables on choosing books: look up a topic (such as 'gorillas') and find lists of books, experts who'll answer questions and even editors who can discuss the subject. Best for kids and schools.

PhoneNetUK   http://www.phonenetuk.bt.com
The free, online equivalent to the old Directory Enquiries.

refdesk.com   http://www.refdesk.com
Check the weather, solve a crossword, do your sums – an impressive collection of links to tools and sites that'll help you out.

Reference.com   http://www.reference.com
Good haystack to start looking for your needle – lets you search newsgroups, mailing lists, and websites in one fell swoop.

Yahoo! Reference   http://dir.yahoo.com/reference/
The best reference sites from Yahoo!'s main catalogue.

Dictionaries and Encyclopedias

A Web of On-line   http://www.facstaff.bucknell.edu/
Dictionaries   rbeard/diction.html
Wordy, worthy and useful: hundreds of bilingual and specialist English dictionaries. Each comes from a different source, so the quality and bias can't always be assured.

AltaVista Translations   http://babelfish.altavista.com
Translate any web page to or from English.

Encarta   http://www.encarta.com
Online version of Microsoft's Encarta encyclopedia. Either search the free concise version (which is good enough for most searches) or subscribe to the deluxe edition – with a seven-day free trial.

Encyclopedia.com   http://www.encyclopedia.com
Free, concise encyclopedia.

ncyclopaedia Britannica http://www.eb.com

> longer to be published in print form, but there's constantly
pdated material on line. A free trial lasts thirty days, then you pay
monthly $5 subscription.

erriam Webster http://www.m-w.com

he general US-English dictionary and thesaurus. Use A Web of
nline Dictionaries for bilingual and specialist English words.

---

uestions Answered

---

sk an expert http://www.askanexpert.com

ot a problem that's bugging you? These very clever people are
aiting eagerly to answer your questions.

sk Jeeves! http://www.askjeeves.com

kay, it's really a search engine, but type in a question and it'll help
ou find the answer quickly.

sk Jeeves for Kids http://www.ajkids.com

k about anything, it'll try to point you to a site that'll tell you
e answer.

formation Please http://www.infoplease.com

ombines dictionaries, encyclopedias, news archives and
ographies. And makes them easy to search.

e Last Word http://www.last-word.com

nswers to your questions from the team at the *New Scientist*. So
hy is the sky blue? Great for children with homework or flum-
oxed parents.

e Why Files http://whyfiles.news.wisc.edu

ere's the answer – especially good on scientific and sports
uestions.

plore http://www.xplore.com

nswers to nagging questions – great for anyone struggling with
eir homework.

Maps and Gazetteers

Active UK Map http://www.ukguide.org/ukmap.htm
Patchy coverage of tourist and community information – but better than nothing.

CIA http://www.odci.gov/cia/publications/factbook
Slightly scary site (with a CIA page for kids and your tacit agreement to be monitored) gives way to the impressively accurate Factbook with world statistics, maps and socioeconomic info.

City Net http://www.city.net
What's going on in cities around the world – aimed at travellers but great for research or homework. Includes local transport, restaurants, guide books, accommodation, sights and customs.

MapQuest http://www.mapquest.com
Search for a place, then plot a map – in extraordinary street-level detail – for the world.

MultiMap http://www.multimap.com
Got a UK phone number? Type it in and get a map of the local area. A neat add-on to the site's core business of providing street-level maps of the UK.

UK Street Map http://www.streetmap.co.uk
Lost in Lewisham? Whip out your laptop, link to your mobile phone, and generate a map centred on any postcode or London street name. Alternatively, ask a passer-by.

Local Information

County Web http://www.countyweb.co.uk
UK-wide local directory for business, sports, attractions, towns and weather arranged by county.

Electronic Yellow Pages http://www.eyp.co.uk
Find a local plumber or order a pizza. You could even splash out and do both.

Town Pages   http://www.townpages.co.uk
Find your local library, swimming pool and civic dump. There's a more comprehensive listings site at http://src.doc.ic.ac.uk/all-uk.html, but it's a little rough on design and navigation.

Yellow Pages   http://www.yell.co.uk
That big yellow book by the phone. Much like Scoot, but not as jolly.

UpMyStreet.com   http://www.upmystreet.co.uk
Ground-breaking site that provides all your local school and government information – and a catalogue of your area's house prices. Often very slow, but persevere.

//SCIENCE AND DISCOVERY

Since the Internet started off as a science project for the military and developed as a medium to exchange scientific findings, it's no surprise that there are hundreds of thousands of sites dedicated to science and discovery. Universities as well as government and military research labs are generous in sharing their research and data. Poke around at the NASA site and you'll find the latest pictures of the galaxy as used by their own scientists. At the other end of the spectrum, consumer sites repackage the language of science into palatable chunks. And kids will love the interactive museum sites – full of buttons to push and levers to pull.

Starting Points

The Last Word   http://www.last-word.com
Answers to your questions from the team at the *New Scientist*. So why is the sky blue? Great for children with homework or flummoxed parents.

Discover Magazine   http://www.discover.com
Science and technology repackaged into palatable, reader-friendly features.

Tomorrow's World   **http://www.bbc.co.uk/tw/**
Auntie charges into the future with the help of the TW team.

News and discovery

National Geographic   **http://www.nationalgeographic.com**
High adventure and scientific discovery melded together.

Nature   **http://www.nature.com**
Academic magazine that provides a forum for announcements of
scientific discoveries. Nonscientists will find the *New Scientist* site
far easier to read.

New Scientist   **http://www.newscientist.com**
Clear and impartial scientific coverage.

ScienceDaily   **http://www.sciencedaily.com**
The latest discoveries from universities and labs around the world.

Scientific American   **http://www.sciam.com**
Well-written articles explaining discoveries.

SciTech Daily   **http://www.scitechdaily.com**
Daily news reporting advances in science with links to journals
and papers.

Smithsonian Magazine's   **http://www.**
Kids' Castle   **kidscastle.si.edu**
Fun twist on science: packed with interesting articles, games and
features on science, history, discovery and art.

Too Cool For Grownups   **http://www.tcfg.com**
Explore space, find out how things work and learn lots in the
process.

Science

ArchNet   **http://archnet.uconn.edu**
Dig up gems from a library of online archaeology resources.

Centre for Alternative Technology http://www.cat.org.uk

Eco-friendly use of power – from solar panels to a green washing machine.

Dinosauria http://www.dinosauria.com

Prehistoric beasts in all their glory. Particularly popular with little boys of all ages.

Fun Science Gallery http://www.funsci.com

Build your own microscope from toilet rolls, and similar ideas for building scientific machines and equipment with household objects.

Science http://www.exploratorium.edu/
Explorer science_explorer/

Chemical reactions in a teacup and other experiments to do at home with household items – simple step-by-steps and clear illustrations.

Science Learning Network http://www.sln.org

How the world works – a dozen museums, forums and features to encourage children to investigate.

Science Museum http://www.nmsi.ac.uk

Plenty of buttons to press and levers to pull at this playful site. Packed high with guides, pictures and video clips of our scientific milestones.

The Natural History Museum http://www.nhm.ac.uk

School coach trips are banished as you surf past the blue whale and dinosaurs. Visitors can pose questions to the experts in this enjoyable learning experience.

The Why Files http://whyfiles.news.wisc.edu

Clear explanations of the science behind news stories and events – from mad-cow disease to genetics.

Space and astronomy

Asteroid & Comet Impact http://impact.arc.nasa.gov
Worry yourself silly with the thought that an asteroid or comet
could hit the Earth and lead to our total destruction.

Astronomy Magazine http://www.astronomy.com
What's in the sky and how to see it.

Bradford Robotic Telescope http://www.telescope.org
Not too much on the telescope, but very readable guide to the way
that stars, galaxies and suns work.

Earth and http://www.fourmilab.ch
moon viewer earthview/vplanet.htm
Real pictures of the Earth and moon; use the nifty navigators to
change your position and see the shadows move.

Johnson Space Center http://www.jsc.nasa.gov
News from the space shuttle and its experiments. For the big
picture on space exploration, visit the main NASA site (www.
nasa.gov).

Mars Exploration http://mpfwww.jpl.nasa.gov
See what the Pathfinder probe saw when it visited Mars.

NASA http://www.nasa.gov
Big-budget space exploration clearly explained.

Space Telescope Science Institute http://oposite.stsci.edu
See what NASA scientists are watching in the sky with pictures from
Hubble and the NASA telescopes.

Star Stuff http://www.starstuff.com
Spot Saturn rising and identify planets and galaxies.

This Week's Sky http://www.skypub.com
at a Glance sights/sights.htm
Don't guess: see for sure what's in the sky tonight.

SHOPPING

he Internet can help you save time and money by bringing just
bout every major shop and tiny specialist boutique to your home.
's fast, convenient, fuss-free and cheap. The larger sites are able
o offer discounts that astonish old-fashioned shoppers. The
ookstores alone slash their prices by half on bestselling titles. And,
: you are looking for expensive, high-margin items, from designer
lothes to consumer electronics, you can – at best – expect to pay
ıst a quarter of the high-street price.

1 this section we cover the most interesting and established of the
hopping sites. If you're looking for a particular product – such as
ooks, music or videos – try the specialist chapter in this book. And
or an in-depth view of hundreds of the best places to shop take a
ook at the sister book **The Virgin Internet Shopping Guide**.

Top tips for safe shopping

enter your credit card and personal details only on a secure
site (one that has the closed-padlock icon in the bottom
line of the browser).

shop only with companies that provide a full contact
address and phone number.

try to stick to shops you know or can phone to check that
they exist.

ensure that delivery costs to your country are made clear
before you order.

keep a note of the transaction number.

request delivery by recorded post or courier so that missing
shipments can be traced.

if a package is damaged, refuse to accept it and call the
company.

8   make sure that you have rights of return on faulty or damaged goods.

9   ensure that, if you're expecting new goods, you receive them rather than a used product.

10 be very, very cautious before bidding on auction sites – try to get a guarantee (some dealers offer them) or pay by credit card.

Finding the Best Price

To help you get the best deal, use one of the comparison tools that scour a bunch of online shops for the lowest prices. The biggest bargain-hunting sites are in the US, but they're on their way to Europe with the arrival of ShopGuide and MyTaxi.

Bottom Dollar   http://www.bottomdollar.com
Brilliant US-based site that lets you compare prices on a great range of products (not just the usual books and CDs). It's as fast and powerful as MySimon, but its design is rather less jolly.

Buy.co.uk   http://www.buy.co.uk
Find the cheapest electricity, gas or other utility – and it's a good directory of shops on the web. Alternatively, try Kura (www.kura.co.uk) or MoneySupermarket (www.moneysupermarket.com) to find the cheapest gas or electricity supplier.

BuyBuddy   http://www.buybuddy.com
Scour the web for the cheapest place to buy books, computers or home goods.

ComputerPrices   http://www.ComputerPrices.co.uk
Helps you find the cheapest computer kit in the UK. Compare these with US prices at BuyBuddy (www.buybuddy.com).

DealPilot   http://www.dealpilot.com
Helps find the cheapest book, video or CD on the market.

Kelkoo   http://www.kelkoo.com
Fast, efficient, comprehensive tool to help find the cheapest supplier on the web.

MySimon   http://www.mysimon.com
One of the best from the US. Send dedicated bargain hunter Simon off to scour the shelves of over 1,200 shops and report back.

MyTaxi   http://www.mytaxi.co.uk
Impressive UK-specific shopping tool to help find the cheapest book, video or CD – plus a good directory of shops.

Shopgenie   http://www.shopgenie.com
Fast, easy-to-use site that compares prices from the biggest online shops to find the cheapest books, videos, and CDs.

ShopSmart   http://www.shopsmart.com
The bargain finder's guide to the UK – fast, well designed and easy to use; great for comparing prices. Lists one thousand stores selling music, books, DVDs and videos, games and computer hardware. Includes gift-finder feature.

Virgin Unlimited   http://www.virginunlimited.com
Ask for absolutely anything, and they'll supply it at a discount price. Use a Virgin Visa card and they'll give you money back too.

Yahoo!   http://www.yahoo.com
Lets you search for goods from people that have setup their own Yahoo! store or the major stores on the web; US based.

Shopping Centres

BarclaySquare   http://www.barclaysquare.co.uk
Fewer than a dozen shops tucked under the safe shopping umbrella of Barclays Bank. Notable are InterFlora and NME's CD shop.

EnterpriseCity   http://www.enterprisecity.co.uk
Friendly guide to UK shops that provide secure order forms (see ShopSmart for UK price comparisons).

ShoppersUniverse http://www.shoppersuniverse.co.uk

Neat, simple mall with over two dozen well-known shops. Or visit ShopSmart and find independent sites.

Auctions

Auction Guide http://www.auctionguide.com

Going, going, go for it – neat guide to online auctions around the world. For a similar idea, but a different approach, try the Auction Channel (http://www.theauctionchannel.co.uk), which combines traditional auction-house sales into one site.

eBay http://www.ebay.com

The mother of all auction sites, with hundreds of thousands of items for sale. Bid from around the world – but check with the vendor on shipping costs.

Ebid http://www.ebid.co.uk

Great-looking site, but not much going on – QXL still wins on activity.

E-swap http://www.eswap.co.uk

Not a swap-shop, but a nice personal auction site. The busiest sections are the computer and music gear for sale; good but not quite up to QXL.

QXL http://www.qxl.co.uk

Buy or sell goodies at the top UK auction site. Unlike the other auction sites, QXL sells gear itself, as well as allowing anyone to sell their belongings in personal auctions.

//SPORTS

What could be less sporty than sitting in front of a computer looking at a screen and clicking a mouse? Yet the Internet is full of excellent sports sites run by teams, organisations and fans. You can stick to the official zones for slick design and lots of nice pictures, or head off towards the amateur fanzines for their infectious enthusiasm.

Any true fan will revel in the statistical information – results, analysis and archives held in databases all over the web. There are vast database-driven websites that concentrate on reports and results, and fanzines for endless analysis. If you missed a match – be it baseball or billiards – there's a site with a report and the final scores. And commentary. And pictures. And often video clips.

Enough about sportsmen and sportswomen: use the web to help you to train, swim, play tennis or scuba-dive. The bigger sites include comprehensive databases of courses, pitches, banks and grounds, each rated to help you find the best place to play tennis, fish, ride or kick a ball.

Starting Point

Sports Illustrated for Kids   http://www.sikids.com
Sports news and results repackaged for kids.

Football

Fantasy League   http://www.fantasyleague.com
Pit your managerial talents against others in a bid to win up to £10,000. There are hundreds of small, free (or cheap) enthusiast sites with their own fantasy leagues, but this is one of the best (and most expensive, at up to £25 per season).

FA Premiership   http://www.fa-premier.com
Official site for the league, but try Unofficial Football Network or Football365 for the smell of the turf.

Football365   http://www.football365.co.uk
Footie trivia, stories, results and analysis – all with a larf.

Footballpages   http://www.footballpages.com
Links to every UK team, in every division, with their official and unofficial fansites.

Footie Search http://tw-net.winsocket.com/fsearch/
The place to find your team's official and unofficial sites.

SoccerAge http://www.soccerage.com
A world perspective on football with video clips of spectacular GOOOAAALLLSSS!

Soccernet http://www.soccernet.com
More gossip and enthusiasm than SoccerAge, but without the video clips.

Teamtalk http://www.teamtalk.com
Home in on your team and get swamped with news, fixtures, stats, players and betting.

Ultimate Soccer Page http://www.angelfire.com/sc/englandA/
Obsessive fan documents every match and result of the national squad – since 1872!

Unofficial Football Network http://www.ufn.co.uk
Transfer talk, unofficial news and speculation are the staple diet for hungry fans.

When Saturday Comes http://www.dircon.co.uk/wsc/
Opinionated views and scurrilous gossip with the latest team talk and results from the team at WSC.

Sports Guides

Aggressive Skating http://www.aggressive.com
Rad baggy-trousered teens should point their inline skates this way.

All England Lawn Tennis http://www.wimbledon.com
Tennis at Wimbledon and little else.

CricInfo http://www.cricinfo.org
A beautifully mown, level pitch. Bring your own tea to enjoy all the information, results and features you could wish for.

Cricket Unlimited http://www.cricketunlimited.co.uk
Combining commentary from the *Guardian*'s team of cricket

reporters with facts and reports from Wisden make this hard to beat. On a level wicket with CricInfo.

fishing   http://www.fishing.co.uk
Where to fish and buy your equipment in this magazine-style site.

Freestyle Frisbee   http://www.frisbee.com
Now you're a web junkie, you'll need to master the basic sport: frisbee.

Golf Today   http://www.golftoday.co.uk
Golf from a (mostly) European perspective – but still has news from worldwide tournaments and a directory of courses. For similar coverage but with a US accent, try Golf.com at http://www. golf.com/.

International Table Tennis Federation   http://www.ittf.com
Whatever you do, don't call it ping-pong.

ITV-F1   http://www.itv-f1.com
The official site for Formula 1 racing from the licence-holding official TV station. Yes, it really is official.

Martial Arts Global   http://www.martial-arts.shoto.com
Improve your karate chop with techniques and schools around the world.

Rugby Football Union   http://www.rfu.com
Official news on the national squad and its matches.

Scrum.com   http://www.scrum.com
Rugger talk and play. For the official line, visit the RFU (www. rfu.com).

Specialized   http://www.specialized.com
Cool dudes who make cool mountain bikes have a cool site, featuring lots of trails for stump-jumping action around the world – with plenty in the UK.

SportsWeb   http://www.sportsweb.com
All the major sports, with plenty of local and world news.

The Tennis Server http://www.tennisserver.com
How to get ahead in tennis. Loads of features and advice.

The Where to Fish Directory http://www.where-to-fish.com
Where you can fish, in Britain and abroad. Over 3,000 pages cover streams, courses, sites and pits. For a specialist guide to fishing in gravel pits, try www.fisheries.co.uk.

Triathlete http://www.triathletemag.com
Just reading the training schedules will make you feel faint. For those who compete, there are plenty of fitness and training regimes, plus results.

//TOYS

Toy shops are launching on to the Internet at a fantastic rate. Vast department stores provide a better range than you would ever see on the high street. And with international delivery it's almost impossible to sell out of this year's Christmas must-have.

British toy shops are rather disappointing on range – generally around a thousand items seems the norm – but at least there's cheap delivery. The biggest, brashest and busiest sites are in the US – FAO Schwartz and Toysmart have astonishing ranges from wooden toys to Barbie dolls – and both will ship back to the UK. Most of the shops include guides for parents (or grandparents) hunting for a suitable toy. If you know what you want, you could visit a specialist shop, such as Letter Box for wooden toys or Lego for, unsurprisingly, Lego.

Starting Points

FAO Schwarz http://www.fao.com
Wonderful toy store, beautifully designed – not quite the scale of its rival etoy.com (but they won't ship outside the US) – plenty of exclusives and shipping around the world.

Funstore.co.uk http://www.funstore.co.uk

Nice shop, but there's only a modest range of toys, even though it's organised with the help of Hamleys – however, confused parents can use the personal helper to find the perfect toy.

Toysmart.com http://www.toysmart.net

Vast range of over 10,000 educational toys for kids from birth and up (start 'em young) – shipped from the US around the world.

Toy Shops

A2Z Beanie Babies http://www.a2zbeaniebabies.co.uk

The whole range of Babies available online.

Ace Toys http://www.toy.co.uk

Mad keen on toys? You'll love this site – all the latest news and gossip.

Acme Toys http://www.acmetoys.com

Vintage toys with a TV or cartoon pedigree – mostly high-quality collectibles out of reach of pocket-money budgets.

Action Man Island Command http://www.actionman.com

Kit out your action hero and play adventure games.

Alberon Dolls and Teddy Bears http://www.dollycrafts.co.uk

High-quality, high-value dolls and teddies that are way too nice for small, sticky paws.

Archie McPhee http://www.mcphee.com

Oddball toys and gifts – the bendy men, children's cat alarm clocks, sumo-wrestler fan for hot summer days.

Barbie.com http://www.barbie.com

The girl with the perfect smile gets her own site – buy a custom-made doll or clothe the one you have. And, yes, there is an exclusive Internet Barbie.

Bargain Beanies   http://www.bargainbeanies.com
Cut-price Beanie Babies – with a good selection of quaintly named 'retireds' (that's second-hand).

Bearworld   http://www.bearworld.co.uk
Bears in every shape and form – including over 50 versions of Po, Tinky Winky and gang (Tubby beanie bags, radios, talking models ... you get the idea).

Brain waves   http://www.brainwaves.co.uk
Toys, videos and games to tease the brain into action.

Character   http://www.
Warehouse Ltd   character-warehouse.com
Barney, Noddy, Bananas in Pyjamas, Rosie and Jim and the usual TV suspects available in games, puzzles, toys – even wallpaper – for mad-keen kids.

Dawson & Son   http://www.dawson-and-son.com
Step back to preplastic days with these wooden puzzles, blocks, toys, dolls' houses and jigsaws.

Lego World   http://www.legoworld.com
Build your own world with the full range from Lego Technic or see the mother site at www.lego.co.uk.

Letter Box   http://www.l-box.com
Home of spinning tops, rocking horses and traditional toys.

Mail Order Express   http://www.mailorderexpress.co.uk
Good range of toys on offer, and a nice feature that'll give you a list of gifts for a certain price. But there are no descriptions, photos or clues as to what half the stuff is.

Naturaltoys.com   http://www.naturaltoys.com
A huge range of natural (mostly wooden) toys that look good for the parents and are fun for the children – ships around the world from the US.

ed Rocket http://www.redrocket.com

eed inspiration? Jump on the Rocket for great ideas – backed up ith a vast selection of trusty playthings. They'll even wrap and ip the toy anywhere in the world.

mart Kids Toys http://www.smartkidstoys.com

reative, fun but challenging toys for children; great range, lots of elp choosing the perfect toy – and free wrapping before it's ipped from Connecticut around the world.

oy Chest http://www.toychest.co.uk

oys for the preschool set – the lucky little things.

oys Я Us http://www.toysrus.co.uk

he warehouse toy shop hits the web walking – reasonable choice, w prices.

oy Town http://www.toytown.co.uk

oys (mostly outdoor fun) for toddler to teenager with good escriptions and pictures to help confused parents decide.

10//FAQS – FREQUENTLY ASKED QUESTIONS

As you start to use the Internet you're bound to come across questions, worries and problems. Many of these are dealt with in the relevant chapter in the main part of the book; for example, if you want to find out how to limit access to unsavoury sites, look to Chapter 3.

In this section, we've covered the most commonly asked questions and their answers.

//THE CONNECTION

Q Why can't I connect?
A You've checked your modem's plugged in and switched on. Make sure that you have typed in the correct user name and password and are dialling the right telephone number.

Q Why does my modem keep dialling?
A Whenever you start a bit of Internet software (your web browser or email program), it automatically tries to connect to the Internet. If it can't connect, or the number's busy, it will redial a few times (normally five times).

Q Why do I keep getting disconnected from the net?
A It's likely that the idle time-out feature is cutting in. This will automatically disconnect you if the computer has not been used for a few minutes. Typically, this happens if you dash off to make a cup of tea or, more likely, you are reading a page without updating or browsing. Open the Control Panel and open the Internet Connections icon; now change the 'Disconnect if idle for x minutes' setting. It's also worth changing the same setting in the modem driver: in the Control Panel, open the Modems icon and click on the Properties button.

The other problem is that your telephone line may have the Call Waiting feature – this will upset your connection and might disconnect you (call your phone company to find out how to disable the feature). Lastly, make sure that someone else in the house isn't picking up a receiver to make an outgoing call when you're online – this, too, will disconnect you.

Q Why isn't my modem working at top speed?
A First, make sure that you have the newest driver software for the modem. You may also find that there's a Flash upgrade for your modem. Visit your modem manufacturer's website and download and install the driver or upgrade. For good advice on upgrades, try either http://www.modem.com or http://www.modemhelp.com.

Q Is it likely that modems will run any faster than their current 56Kbps?
A Probably not. That is, not really over a normal telephone line. In fact, it's actually illegal in the US to run a modem at 56Kbps (the maximum allowable is 53Kbps). Modems will gradually die off as cable modems, ADSL and other digital communications come into place.

Q Will my free ISP account last for ever?
A It should do – but most free ISPs check that you've used your account on a regular basis. If you don't use the service for ninety days, they will probably cancel your account and you'll have to reregister.

Q How do I cancel my account?
A Check your contract with the ISP. Some will require a month's notice, others won't. Visit your ISP's main website and check the email address for the admin department. Send them an email telling them you want to cancel your account – and ask for an email to acknowledge this.

Q What's the best time to go online?
A Depends what's important to you. The cheapest time (in

telephone costs) is evenings and weekends. The busiest time (and so the time when the web is slowest) is evenings and weekends. For top speed, connect when the US is asleep.

//BROWSING

Q Why does my web browser keep crashing?
A It shouldn't. This probably means that you're not using the latest version of the browser. As new ways of enhancing web pages are developed, older browsers can find it hard to manage and simply stop working. Visit www.microsoft.com or www.netscape.com to download the latest version of your browser.

Q Why isn't a website there any more?
A The website may have been closed down or, more likely, the designer has redesigned the site and reorganised the way the pages are stored and given them new names. If a page doesn't work, visit the main site's home page.

Q I sometimes see 'Error 404' or 'Error, page not found'. What does it mean?
A It means that the address of a web page does not exist. Either you typed in the wrong address or the site has been redesigned and the names of the web pages have been changed.

Q Do all web-page addresses start with the letters 'www'?
A No. You'll often see addresses that look very odd but will still work fine. The way addresses are created is slowly changing, so you can expect to see more addresses that are just names.

Q I find the typeface far too small on many of my favourite web pages. Any solutions?
A You can increase the default, standard size of fonts used by your web browser by choosing View/Font Size or pressing Ctrl-] to increase the size (and Ctrl-[to decrease the size).

Q What's a secure connection? How can I get one?
A Secure connections are set up by the web server (not by your

veb browser) – you can tell you've got a secure connection
vhen the tiny closed-padlock icon is displayed at the bottom of
he screen.

**I saved some images from a website to my hard disk. Now how
an I view these GIF and JPEG format files on my PC?**
A The simplest method is to use your web browser as the viewer.
tart your browser (choose not to connect and to work offline);
tart Windows Explorer. Click and drag one of the images from
xplorer on to the browser and you'll see it displayed. The
lternative is to use a paint program that's better than Paint
nstalled with Windows. Try Paintshop Pro (http://www.jasc.com) or
earch www.filez.com for a wide selection.

What's a plug-in?
A A plug-in is a special bit of software that adds a new feature to
our web browser. For example, if you want to view video or
nimation in your browser, it needs to have a plug-in that supports
his. If you visit a site that uses snazzy multimedia tricks and you
lon't have the right plug-in, you'll be told and given the chance to
lownload the file required.

**I want to use bitmap images I created on my PC on my own web
age. How can I do this?**
A You can, generally, use only GIF and JPEG graphics files on a
veb page. You'll need to use an image-editor program to convert
our BMP format files to either GIF or JPEG. Try Paintshop Pro
http://www.jasc.com) or search Filez (http://www.filez.com).

I've been told to clean out my cache – why?
A Your cache (pronounced 'cash') is a folder where your web
prowser temporarily stores the images and text files for the web
page it's visiting. Most web browsers set aside tens of megabytes
f hard disk space for the cache so that they can store thousands of
veb pages. The advantage is that next time you visit the page, the
prowser will pull up the files from your hard disk rather than from

the slow web link. If your browser seems to run very slowly, your cache may be too big or too full.

Choose the Options/Network Preferences menu in Netscape or View/Options/Advanced for IE users. You can now adjust the size of your cache (don't make it any bigger than 15–20Mb), or clear it.

Q I have downloaded a file that ends in the ZIP extension. Why does nothing happen when I double-click to run it?
A A ZIP file contains a compressed version of the original file(s) that has been squeezed down to save space and time when downloading. To unzip your file, you'll need an unzip program. The best known is WinZip from www.winzip.com.

Q When I try to save a page with the File/Save As option in my browser, it just saves the text and layout. How can I get the graphics as well?
A You need to use an offline browser that will grab all the associated files and store them on your hard disk. Try WebWhacker (http://www.webwhacker.com).

Q I have visited a few sites that play music samples and I would like to save these to my hard disk to play back later. How do I do this?
A Most music is stored in the WAV, MIDI, MP3 or RealAudio formats. To download and save any of these files, right-click on the link that plays the file and select Save Link As.

Q Should I be worried about cookies?
A No, they are normally perfectly harmless. Most big sites use a cookie (it's a little file on your hard disk that lets a website store information on your machine) to store your name or preferences or the last time that you visited the site.

Q I download lots of files from the Internet. I always check these with my virus scanner before I run the program, but what do I do with a compressed ZIP file?
A When you unzip the contents of a ZIP file, it won't start any virus

that's present; this means you can safely unzip the files and then run your normal virus scanner on the resulting files. However, if you're nervous about doing even this, you can ask the splendid WinZip utility (www.winzip.com) to scan the contents of a ZIP file before you open it up. Choose the Options/Program Locations menu in WinZip and enter the name of your virus scanning software. Now you can scan ZIP files from the Actions menu.

Q How can I be sure to download a file as quickly as possible?
A If you are downloading a file from a commercial site, such as CNET, you'll be given a list of various sites that store this file. You could choose the nearest geographic site, or use lateral thinking and pick a site in the world where it's still night-time – the traffic will be much lighter and your download should fly.

Q Can I catch a virus by looking at a web page?
A Viewing images, entering information in a form or just viewing text on a web page is perfectly harmless. That means 99 per cent of all websites are fine. Sometimes, you'll visit a website that uses snazzy multimedia or other trickery. You may be warned that your web browser needs to download a plug-in or Java or ActiveX applet (the name for a little program). These applets are normally developed to provide extra functions – such as shopping carts, multimedia or special effects. However, it is possible to write nasty little applets that trash the files on your computer. To avoid this, don't accept plug-in downloads from sites where you don't know the company.

Q Can I stop my kids viewing porn online?
A Yes, almost totally. Use one of the parental control programs such as NetNanny (www.netnanny.com) or CyberSitter (www.cybersitter.com) or, if you're on AOL, click on their Parental Control page. However, the best advice is to move the computer to the sitting room, where everyone can see it and make sure you're in the room when they're on the computer. They'll be too embarrassed to view anything naughty! See Chapter 3 for more details.

//EMAIL

Q How do I set up my computer so that each member of the family gets their own email address?
A Make sure that you choose an ISP that provides multiple email accounts (normally called POP3 accounts). For example, Freeserve, Virgin Net and AOL each provide five email accounts to share among your family.

Q Why does an email get returned as 'undeliverable'?
A You've typed in the wrong email address when you created the message. Check that you have their correct address – it should be in two parts: their name or nickname, an '@' symbol and their company or ISP name. Some addresses have full stops or underscore (_) symbols – make sure you type these in as well.

Q What can I do about junk mail?
A Unsolicited commercial junk mail – called spam – is a bane of email life. You waste precious time downloading messages offering you deals you don't want. Many ISPs now have anti-spam systems in place that automatically recognise known culprits and reject any mail received from them. Alternatively, if you keep getting junk mail from a particular address, you can create a new filter (or rule) in your email program that automatically deletes any message from this person as soon as it's received. To avoid getting junk mail in the first place, don't use your real email address when posting messages on newsgroups, in chat sessions or in discussion groups.

Q Can anyone else read the emails I send?
A Email messages are sent in plain text form – as you typed it out. As the email passes across the Internet, malicious system managers could, in theory, read it. However, with hundreds of millions of mail messages zipping around the net every day, it's unlikely. You can scramble the contents of your messages. The most secure system around is called PGP (**http://www.pgp.com**), although most email programs have some form of encryption built in.

Q What do I do if someone's harassing me by email?
A Tread carefully. If it's an unknown nut, it may be better not to reply (this can wind them up even more); change your email address – get a free account – and tell your ISP that you've been getting this type of email. They are in a better position to try to track down the sender and automatically block any further email.

//NEWSGROUPS AND CHAT

Q Will I get junk mail if I post a message to a newsgroup?
A Some unscrupulous companies comb the newsgroups to pick up the email addresses of users, then sell these on as mailing lists, so you may well get junk mail. If your ISP provides you with more than one email address (most do), reserve one for your newsgroup activity and ditch any unwanted mail received on that address.

Q I posted a message a few days ago, but now it's gone. Why?
A So many messages are posted every day that your ISP's computer has to delete messages after a few days to save space.

Q How can I search for old newsgroup messages?
A You need to use one of the archive sites – such as Deja (www.deja.com) – which store copies of messages from all newsgroups

//GLOSSARY

Address (email) Unique name that identifies a person and lets you send them a mail message. Written in the form 'response@virgin-pub.co.uk'.

address (website) The unique location of a site on the web. Sometimes called a URL (uniform resource locator).

address book A list of names and their email addresses. Your email program provides this feature to let you manage your contacts.

ADSL (asymmetric digital subscriber line) New system of transferring information over a standard telephone cable at very high speeds – several thousand times faster than a modem. See also ISDN below.

alias An alternative name you use either in chat or email.

antivirus program Special software that detects and removes viruses from programs and documents. You should run an antivirus program on any file you download from the Internet or receive via email.

attachment A file sent with an email message.

authoring Creating a web page.

backbone The high-speed communication lines that link up the ISPs around the world and provide the foundation of the Internet.

bit A basic storage unit used in computers; a bit can be one of only two values: 1 or 0. Data is stored in a computer as a combination of bits (eight, see byte). Bits are normally used when specifying the transmission speed of a modem (for example, 56Kbps means 56,000 bits sent every second).

body The main text part of an email message.

bookmark A way of storing the address of an interesting website in your web browser. When you want to revisit the site, just click on the bookmark entry. Microsoft calls this feature 'Favorites'.

bounce An email message returned to the sender because it was sent to an invalid address.

bps Bits per second.

broken link A hyperlink that doesn't work when you click on it. You'll see the 'Error 404' or 'Error, page not found' warning messages.

browser Special software that you need to view a web page and navigate through the web. The two main browsers are Netscape Navigator and Microsoft Internet Explorer.

byte A basic unit for storing data in a computer. A byte is made up of eight separate bits and can store numbers between 0 and 255. Your computer's memory and hard-disk storage capacity are normally measured in bytes. Compare this with bit.

cache Way of (temporarily) storing the last few web pages you have visited so that next time you visit the page, you save time and avoid downloading the images again. This is a feature of your web browser and controlled automatically.

CC (carbon copy) Field just below the address field 'To:' that lets you type in the address of another person who should see a copy of this message. The person in the 'To:' field will be told that copies have been sent.

CGI (common gateway interface) An advanced feature of website programming that allows a web page to send information to a program running on the server. See also Perl.

chat System that lets you type out messages that are seen instantly by other users, unlike newsgroups (where you pin up a message in a forum). See also instant messaging and Internet relay chat.

client Your computer. Compare this with mail server below.

compression Special way of squeezing a file so that it's smaller and so takes less time to download. You'll need special software to decompress (or 'unzip') the file before you can use it.

cookie A piece of information stored on your hard disk by a website – it lets the website store information to help it keep track of you.

dial-up A connection to the Internet that is not permanent: you need to dial a number to make the connection (just like using a normal phone). If you get an account with an ISP, it's usually a dial-up account – this means you can get online using a modem.

directory A website that contains a list of other websites, normally organised into sections and often with a search feature. Yahoo! (**www.yahoo.co.uk**) is one of the best-known directories.

Domain name The unique name that identifies one website or computer on the Internet. For example, the domain name 'microsoft.com' identifies the server provided by Microsoft.

domain-name system (DNS) A method of converting the domain name to the IP (Internet protocol) address (a series of numbers) that's actually used to locate the computer. The list of names and addresses are stored on a domain-name server (also called DNS). See also IP below.

download To transfer a file from a distant computer on to your own, via the Internet.

email Electronic mail. Way of sending text messages, files and video clips to another user on the Internet.

emoticons See smiley.

encryption A way of scrambling a message or contents of a file so that only the intended recipient can unscramble it and read it. When you visit a 'secure website' it uses an encryption system to ensure that any information you type in is scrambled as it is transferred over the Internet.

FAQ Frequently asked question. FAQs are often to be found on websites as an aid to visitors.

Favourite Often spelled the American way: favorite. See bookmark.

filter A special feature of email software that lets you automatically manage and move messages into folders according to key words in the message.

firewall A special security system (normally installed in a company) that lets users in the company access the Internet, but prevents outside hackers gaining access to the company's computers.

forward A feature of email software that lets you send a message you've received to another user.

freeware Software that can be used on a permanent basis without charge.

ftp (file transfer protocol) Protocol used to transfer files between computers over the Internet.

gateway A link between two different systems. For example, an email gateway can be used to resend an email message to a fax machine or pager.

GIF A common graphics format used for images.

gopher An older system that allowed users to navigate the Internet – it's now been almost entirely replaced by the web.

header The part of an email message that contains the recipient's address, sender's name, subject of the message and any delivery options.

home page The first page you see when you visit a website, before proceeding to other documents and links. The home page is normally stored in a file called 'index.html'.

HTML (hypertext markup language) The set of codes that are used to lay out and format a web page. These codes let you add links, define text styles, use colours and insert images into a page.

HTTP (hypertext transfer protocol) The series of commands (protocol) used by a web browser to ask an Internet server for a particular web page. You'll see this at the start of most web addresses (though you don't have to type it in) to identify this address as a web page rather than a file (which uses a sister protocol, FTP).

hypertext A way of connecting web pages together across the web. One word or image in a page can be linked (this facility is often called a hyperlink) to any other page on the site or on any other site on the web. When the user clicks on the link, they jump immediately to the referenced page. It's the way you browse and surf the web.

IE (Internet Explorer) Microsoft's web-browser software.

instant messaging A facility that lets you know the moment a friend has connected to the Internet and is available for a natter. When you type in a message, it is sent instantly to the other user and is a bit like a text-based equivalent of a phone call. See also Internet relay chat.

Internet or net The millions of computers that are linked together around the world so that each can communicate with another or others. The Internet is public, so any user can visit any other computer linked to it. See Chapter 1 for a full definition and history of the net.

Internet Explorer (IE) Microsoft's web browser software.

Internet relay chat (or IRC) A vast collection of chat rooms (called channels); using special software (that's free to download), you can join a channel and chat to any other people who are there.

Internet Service Provider (ISP) A company that provides a doorway on to the Internet for you, the user. When you subscribe, you'll get a set of telephone-access numbers (called the POPs), which your modem can dial to link to the Internet. Most ISP companies provide access numbers in one area or country; a few provide global access numbers. If the ISP also publishes its own information for its users, it's called a content provider.

intranet A mini, private Internet within a company. Employees can browse their company information in just the same way as you would on an Internet using a web browser.

IP (Internet protocol) The key to the way computers on the Internet can locate each other and communicate. An IP address is a string of numbers that identifies each of the main server computers on the Internet. To make it easier for users to manage an IP address, it's translated into a friendlier text form, called a domain name. See also domain-name system above.

ISDN (integrated services digital network) A high-speed digital version of your standard old phone line. You'll get a speedy connection to the Internet using an ISDN link, but you need a special modem (called a terminal adapter) and an ISP that provides ISDN access for its users. See also ADSL.

ISP See Internet Service Provider.

Javascript A special programming language that lets web-page designers enhance the basic effects provided by HTML.

JPEG A file format used to store the graphic images displayed on a web page; JPEG files are usually used for photographic images, while GIF files (see above) are better for simple images with fewer colours.

Kbps (kilobits per second) One thousand bits of information sent every second – used to measure the speed of a modem or other communications device. See also bit.

keyword A word that you type into a search engine to find information.

link See hypertext.

mailbox A special area at your ISP where your incoming mail messages are temporarily stored until you connect to the net, download and read the mail.

mail server A computer on the Internet that deals with your email – storing your incoming mail until you log in and read it and passing on the email messages you send to the right address.

MIME (multipurpose Internet multimedia extensions) A way of sending a file within an email message.

modem A device that connects your computer to a telephone line and allows you to dial and connect to an ISP – and so gain access to the Internet. A modem (short for modulator-demodulator) works by converting your computer's data into sound signals that can be sent along a phone line. New communication systems (such as ISDN, ADSL and cable modems) do away with this conversion and send information in its native digital format to provide much higher transfer speeds.

moderated The term used to describe a newsgroup, chat system or mailing list that is monitored by someone who ensures that the messages are decent or to do with the subject.

name server A special computer on the Internet that converts a domain name to its IP address. See domain-name system.

Netscape Navigator One of the most popular web browsers on the market – get a free copy from **www.netscape.com**.

newsgroup A public discussion forum that lets anyone discuss a particular subject, hobby or interest. There are over 60,000 newsgroups that, collectively, are called Usenet. They provide one of the most active areas of the Internet – you'll need a newsgroup reader (or newsreader) to read and submit messages, but then you'll be hooked.

newsreader Special software you need to access, read and post messages to a newsgroup – both web browsers from Microsoft and Netscape have a newsreader built in.

offline Not connected to the Internet.

online Connected to the Internet, so incurring telephone charges.

Perl A very popular programming language that is used to add advanced features (such as a shopping cart) to a website; the programs run on the server of your ISP, but deliver information back to the user's web browser.

plug-in A special program that works in conjunction with your web browser to provide an extra feature (often multimedia, video or animation) – if you need a plug-in to view a particular web page, you'll be told and given the chance to download the file automatically.

POP (point of presence) A telephone number (provided by your ISP) that your modem dials to connect to the ISP's computer and so to the Internet. Make sure that your ISP provides low-call local numbers.

POP3 A method of transferring email messages over the Internet. The POP3 standard is normally used to retrieve your messages and the SMTP (simple mail-transfer protocol) standard is used to send the mail. See also IMAP.

post office See mail server.

protocol A set of rules that define the way something happens. For example, the POP3 system of sending mail is a protocol that defines the commands used to actually transfer the message.

public-domain Something (either a text or program) that is freely available to anyone to view or try. The copyright remains with the original author.

secure website or server A website where it's safe to type in personal details (such as a credit-card number) – and be sure that the information cannot be intercepted by a hacker 'listening' in. You can tell you are at a secure website because your web browser displays a tiny closed-padlock icon in the bottom status bar.

shareware Software that can be downloaded and tried out for free, but if you plan to use it regularly, you'll need to pay a registration fee.

signature A few lines of text that are automatically added to any email you write or newsgroup message that you post. Your signature could just include your name or provide contact details or company name and slogan.

smiley A facial expression made up of keyboard characters, often added to email or newsgroup postings to add expression or feeling. For instance, a colon, hyphen and closing parenthesis :-) is a smiling face, and means you're happy, or that the sentence was a joke or meant as fun. Sometimes called emoticons.

SMTP (simple mail-transfer protocol) See POP3.

snail mail The old-fashioned method of sending a letter via the Post Office.

spam Unwanted email – normally sent in bulk to advertise something.

SSL (Secure Sockets Layer) A way of scrambling the data between your web browser and the website so that no hacker or eavesdropper can read the information you are sending. Normally used on a web page that asks you to enter a credit-card number or personal details. Your browser will indicate a secure SSL page by displaying a tiny closed-padlock icon in the bottom line of the windows. Don't shop without this!

TCP/IP (Transmission Control Protocol/Internet Protocol) The rules that escribe how all information is sent over the Internet and how it finds its way to the right destination.

elnet A special program that lets you connect to any computer on the Internet and type in commands as if you were sitting in front of the computer. You'll use Telnet only for advanced website management.

ART (Universal Asynchronous Receiver/Transmitter) A special chip in your computer responsible for sending and receiving data in a serial form – that means anything sent via a modem.

RL (uniform resource locator) The correct name for the full address of a web page. For example, 'microsoft.com' is a domain name, 'www. microsoft.com' is the website address for Microsoft and 'www. microsoft. com/index.html' is the URL to the site's home page.

senet The collective name for the mass of over 60,000 newsgroups on the Internet.

uencoding An older method of converting files into a special format before attaching them to an email message. Thankfully, you don't need to do this any more, owing to the arrival of MIME, which automatically sorts out attachments.

VAP (wireless application protocol) A system that lets you access email and the Internet via a mobile phone.

web browser A software program that lets you view a web page and navigate the web.

web page A single, individual page within a website. Each web page is stored in a separate file; the file contains HTML commands that describe the text, its layout, formatting and links.

web server A computer that stores a website (generally, web servers store hundreds of separate websites or, in the case of mammoth sites from the BC or CNN, the website is big enough to deserve its own web server.

website A collection of web pages produced by one person or company or other organisation, and about a particular subject.

Winsock Software that lets your computer communicate with the Internet via a standard dial-up connection; Windows includes a Winsock utility that is configured automatically.

WWW (World Wide Web or W3 or web) The collective name for the millions of individual websites on the Internet.

//INDEX